CRACK IT!

'The future belongs to those who believe in the future of their dreams'

ELEANOR ROOSEVELT

'Whether you think you can, or you think you can't, you're right'

HENRY FORD

'All our dreams can come true if we have the courage to pursue them'

WALT DISNEY

WOW! Inspirational BUSINESS

CRACK IT!

5 STEPS TO CREATING YOUR WOW! CHIROPRACTIC PRACTICE

Jo and Steve Davison

A&F
Alice&Fred Books

A&F
Alice&Fred Books

First published in Great Britain in 2011

This edition published in 2015 by

Alice & Fred Books
Rosden House
Suite 243
372 Old Street
London
EC1V 9AU

British Library Cataloguing in Publication Data
A record of this book is available from the British Library

ISBN: 978-0-9560965-1-7

Book design and typesetting by Andy Ashdown Design
www.andyashdowndesign.co.uk

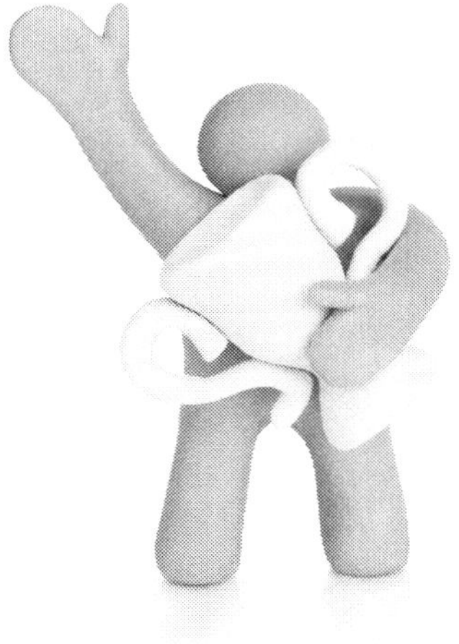

This book is dedicated to all the courageous chiropractic business owners who have dared to step up to achieve their dreams, provide employment for others and spread their chiropractic message to bring hope and joy into the lives of people in their community. We honour and salute you!

To every amazing SHC team member past and present (we are so sorry that there are too many of you to mention personally), please trust we are truly grateful to each one of you for your commitment and contribution so far.
Thank you for being in the 2%.

To our consultancy clients and chiropractors who have attended our seminars so far – thank you for seeking our advice and allowing us to help you on your journey.
We look forward to the next phase with you.

Mick and Margaret, we simply could not have achieved everything in the past ten years without your unconditional love, help and support. Thank you!

Harry and Louis – thank you for your patience and understanding when we sat for what seemed like endless hours at the kitchen table working on this book – the 'blah, blah, blah' stuff we discussed is complete. We hope you will both be inspired to live your dreams.
Lots of love, Mummy and Daddy.

CONTENTS

THEY SAY ANY TIME YOU SEE A TURTLE ON A FENCE POST, YOU CAN BE SURE HE HAD SOME HELP GETTING THERE:

Graham Downing DC
Joe Morley DC
Gerald Turnbull DC
Greg Parkin-Smith DC
Phil Petts DC
Arif Soomro DC
Chuck Gibson DC
Bryn and Terry Chimes DC
Ed Groenhart DC
Mummy Yuho DC
Mark Prudden DC
Rob Walsh
Marie Burton DC
Kevin Burton
Jo Ladd DC
Michael Gerber
David Brewer

Stuart Wiggins
Sue Street
Avnish Goyal
Annabel and Dan Nash

Melissa, Amanda and all the UCA executive team
Marg and Mick Davison
Trina Glibbery

Peter and Julie Boffo
Ann Lancaster
John Lancaster
Sarita and Vijay Gohill
Daniel Priestley
Cherye Roche DC
Gill St Leger
Matt Poulter DC
Dean Blackstock DC
Alex Cover DC
Charlie Herbert DC
Grayson Nolan DC
Amanda North
Emma Whipp
The SHC team
Nic Rixon
Andy Ashdown

And to those who continue to inspire us but don't know us personally (yet!):

Jack Canfield, Mark Victor Hanson, Tony Robbins, Wayne Dyer, Gill Fielding, Fabrizio Mancini DC and John Demartini DC

FOREWORD

I still remember when I first thought of becoming a Chiropractor. It was after being adjusted for the first time in my life and feeling not only less pain in my body, but a clarity in my mind like I never had before. It was like my innate intelligence was awaken and now I could finally see my life's purpose. I want you to think about when was your first thought about becoming a Chiropractor? What did you think it would be like? How did you see yourself spending your days? What quality of life did you feel you would provide for your family?

After being a successful Chiropractor for over 25 years, a president of one of the biggest Chiropractic schools and seminars in the world, helping thousands in our profession be more successful and influencing more people through my books, lectures and media appearances than any Chiropractor alive, one thing I am certain of, is that your practice success has nothing to do with Chiropractic. Our success in practice has to do with your thoughts and behaviours. It is the believe you have as to whether you feel worthy of success, a humbleness to learn from others and a service attitude towards your patients.

I have seen how you can take a chiropractor from an office doing 500 patients a week and put them in an office seeing 100 patients a week and how in less than 6 months, they will be seeing the same amount they were seeing before because of who they are and not only what they do. This book has the essentials of what you need to transform you from where you are to where you want to be. It is packed with examples of people that have done what you may think is impossible. It will share the lessons that we did not get in our Chiropractic schools about how to manage our business. Yes, our business. I know that when you take care of your business, success is sustainable. The fact that Chiropractic care helps people get well is a given. We know it by our experience, our research and the millions of testimonials every year from our patients.

The question is, are you ready for more success? Are you ready to experience what you thought this profession was going to be like when you chose it. Are you ready to learn from 2 of the most successful people in our profession? If the answer is yes, then read this book with complete engagement and urgency. Humanity is struggling more today than ever and by applying the information on this book, you will be in the top percentage of successful Chiropractors around the world that have done it already. Give yourself permission to BE different by shifting your thinking and doing. This book is like a roadmap to what is possible. It is innovative, fresh, real and full of tips on how to do what you need to do.

Congratulations in entering in the space of Success in Chiropractic and I am honored to be in this journey with you. Love, Fab.

Dr. Fabrizio Mancini

INTRODUCTION

This book will change your life. We know. What you're about to read has already changed ours. If you are open-minded and willing to play, if you approach the ideas set down here with passion and enthusiasm, then you will fly! We guarantee it.

Before we go any further, let's introduce ourselves to you. We are Jo and Steve Davison, and our training and consultancy company helps motivated chiropractors build, grow and sustain their own WOW! chiropractic practice.

Ten years ago, we set-up our first chiropractic centre and started an emotional roller-coaster ride into chiropractic business ownership. Our journey has meant that we have experienced the setting up, building and growing of our initial practice, have expanded into multiple sites, employed associates, receptionists, chiropractic assistants, massage therapists, run practices that we worked in and those we didn't. We have lived the highs and lows of chiropractic business ownership and discovered the success strategies that create an ethical, fun, busy, profitable, relationship-generated chiropractic business.

Our journey into speaking, consultancy and training came about a few years ago when we began receiving requests to go and help other chiropractors. We found ourselves working with a mixture of people, some of whom wanted to break free from the not-so-good bits of practice, some who were setting out on their practice ownership journey, and others who were plain burnt-out and wanted 'a new way' of practising. We discovered a passion for helping chiropractors create their own WOW! practice. A practice of their dreams. We love to help chiropractors free themselves from being 'jobbing chiropractors' who happen to *own* the practice (often working harder and getting paid less than they did as associates), living on a knife-edge, stressed and working far too hard to keep it all going, to becoming *chiropractic business owners* and manifesting their dream life; creating opportunities for themselves and those around them. It has been a joy to see life transformations take place for everyday people who realised that they deserved more.

Working with so many chiropractors over the years, as well as through our own practice experience, we have probably seen and dealt with every kind of problem and challenge that chiropractic business owners face today in their endeavour to be successful, to be energised and to build and maintain their own WOW! practice.

Whilst the challenges that chiropractic businesses face are not all exactly the same, they can be bundled (broadly) into three separate groups. There are challenges that the new chiropractic business faces, those that the intermediate practice faces and those that the advanced practice faces.

Whatever the stage of the business, five specific challenges come up time after time. It doesn't really matter where in the world the practice is or at what stage of development. They are:

- To get enough new guests to sustain the chiropractors working in the practice.
- To inspire guests to finish their prescribed care programmes so that they get the very best out of their chiropractic experience.
- To attract and retain a 'dream team'.
- To make more money (ethically), have more time with less stress.
- To avoid burn-out and have an outstanding work/life balance.

In this book we will address all of these challenges. This is the blueprint we used to build a world-class business. A five-step strategy that will bring an abundance of new guests to any practice and allow the chiropractor to walk each and every guest through their prescribed programme of care ethically, honestly and, best of all, joyfully. We reveal a system that builds a unique culture so that chiropractors always attract dream team members and retain only those who are inspired by what they have created. We lay out the principles to create a lifestyle membership system full of chiropractic advocates who love what the practice does and how it does it.

Whilst we cannot include everything in this short book, we hope that it will inspire you to create a practice that fits with your dream, gives you your dream life and helps you achieve your aspirations. In the words of Apple founder, Steve Jobs, we want to help you make your 'dent on the universe'.

We created the chiropractic practice of our dreams. We are not especially bright or insightful or favoured in any special way. We did it on a shoestring in the beginning. If we can, then so can you! We can't wait to help you get started.

If this strikes a chord within you, then welcome along. Those who know us well, those who have worked with us or consulted with us over the last ten years, know that our aim is to transform the way you think, the way you act and ultimately the way you approach chiropractic practice ownership. Our purpose in writing this book is to help create a chiropractic profession filled with passionate, busy, financially secure, ethical chiropractors helping as many people as possible. We want an outstanding chiropractic experience for every guest all over the world. It's our intention that after you have read this book, you will be truly inspired and ready to take action!

Much love – Jo and Steve Davison

HOUSEKEEPING

We have some 'before we start' bits that we want to share with you right away. Stuff that might be confusing unless we explain it first. Our spelling of some words, for instance. We are from the UK and we spell some words a bit differently from other English speakers. 'Center' for example is spelt 'centre' in the UK. We use 's' where other English speakers use 'z'. So 'energize' becomes 'energise' and 'realize' becomes 'realise' and so on.

We also use the word 'guest' for 'patient'. We do this because the word 'guest' is a better fit for us than the word 'patient'. It gels with the way we want to take care of those who come to us. So 'guest' is not a UK thing, it's an 'us' thing. We use the letters PA a lot too. This stands for *personal appearance* (not personal assistant!).

We'd love to hear from you, by the way. If you read this book, if you have taken one of our programmes (note the English spelling of program there!), let us know how you are getting on. We love feedback!

Finally, there are 'Action' sections throughout the book. Please commit to going through them when they pop up. Don't skim past them! We would also encourage you to read the chapters in the way they have been set out. Don't be tempted to skip ahead or 'cherry-pick' parts of the text. It is designed to be taken in the order in which it is written. Apart from all of that, please enjoy!

HAVE YOU EVER FACED THESE CHALLENGES?

Back in 2003, our chiropractic centre was coming up to two years old. We had grown steadily over the formative months, we had taken on team members, we had two chiropractic associates. We had acquired a building, we had bills and wages to pay, and we had overheads to maintain. We were feeling by turns excited and energetic, frustrated or shattered, depressed or elated. It was an emotional roller-coaster ride.

Jo wanted our CAs to do a lot more than just 'turn up' for work. She wanted them to be energised by what we were doing. To be chiropractic advocates. To 'get it'. Apart from one associate who was a gift from God, the rest of the staff didn't seem to get it at all, or if they did, they didn't believe or understand it. They seemed sceptical and behaved as if we wanted them to 'sell a product' which worked for a few lucky guests, but certainly not all.

Jo wanted to work alongside her 'dream team'. Yet they weren't like a team. She felt that she had to do everything herself – adjust guests, sign the cheques, clean the floor. The staff – they were not team back then but staff – would present her with problem after problem to solve. She would happily oblige and so they would present more problems. They relied on her to solve them all. Jo often felt as if she was trying to get a herd of unruly sheep up a hill, not lead an empowered group of positive people. Both she and the associates needed new guests, yet they appeared to drop off care almost as quickly as they started, leaving one of the associates complaining that there were not enough new patients and wanting more. They certainly didn't understand that new guests were a precious commodity who needed to be educated, loved and treasured.

Steve, on the other hand, was challenged by the business of chiropractic. The wages would take hours every month, (the overtime appeared to be like an open cheque book), the bill-paying was a balancing act, and then there was the ordering of supplies, the collating of receipts, invoices and delivery notes, the marketing, the meetings with the accountant and the bank manager. There were many nights when he found himself sitting on the stairs, head in hands, contemplating how we could make it work. On the nights Steve wasn't on the stairs, you could find Jo there instead! The business of practice ownership and the responsibility of ensuring we could pay the staff, took its toll. It was such an effort just keeping it all afloat. Steve knew most practices relied on the chiropractic owner to drive things forward. That if they were out of action so was the practice. This model was outdated. It was not a business model at all. We had not created a business, we had merely created a job for ourselves, where we worked harder and often for less money and more stress than we had as associates. To grow the practice, to get it to the next level, Steve knew he would have to work out how to break that mould.

We were both challenged by 'difficult' guests too. We were fairly newly qualified and just learning our profession. Consequently many guests didn't listen to our advice, or they ignored it, or questioned it; they didn't stick to their programmes of care or they were angry or wanted to take charge.

A life-changing day for Jo came when she had been working hard for days. As well as adjusting, she was doing the 'receptionist's' shift who had called in sick with five minutes to go and no one else would cover. The associates were both on holiday. Jo had the flu. Sick-as-a-dog flu. Rather than cancelling patients, she felt determined to stay and adjust the people who needed her – as if the universe was trying to teach her something. Patient after patient failed to show. They didn't call, and so Jo spent her afternoon adjusting the guests who did show and, in between, lying on the bench in one of the rooms until the next one arrived.

We had a policy written on the wall that said, 'Please give us twenty-four hours' notice if you are unable to make your appointment. Unfortunately we have to charge missed appointments.' We had never used it. However, this day sent Jo to a place where she just could not take it any more. The next time she saw one of the guests who had stood her up that day, she told him he had to pay for the missed session. They ended up getting into a disagreement and he stomped off out of the centre.

Those of you who know Jo will know she is not one for confrontation. However, she had become so burnt-out and stressed that she followed the guest out of the building and found herself shouting at him to come back inside. He was sitting in his convertible on the drive (we also had a sign saying, 'Please do not park on the drive as we like to reserve this for emergency guests' – this sign was always ignored by this particular man). The months spent placating him, encouraging him, putting up with his moaning, his turning up late and firing at her feet, all came to a head, and Jo told him exactly what she thought whilst he sat looking away, pretending to ignore her. Finally he came back inside and wrote a cheque for the missed session. At that moment, Jo realised it had all become too much. She still has that cheque to this day, framed in her office. She never cashed it and keeps it as a reminder of the day that she 'shouted at her guest', and will never allow herself ever to get to that burnt-out place again. That day showed us that things needed to change. The team needed to be inspired to rally to the cause, our lists had to be filled with guests who loved to see us and vice versa. However – and it was a big however – we didn't have a clue how to change any of it. So inevitably things just got worse.

Finally there were two incidents that occurred within quick succession that forced us to make the change. They made us re-examine everything we had ever done up to that point. Not tweak or adjust (pardon the pun) but change everything – and do it radically.

The first incident we later jokingly called 'the stash behind the desk' incident. This was an occasion when Jo had gone behind the front desk and found a stack of folders on the bottom shelf – a stack of clinical notes. Jo thought they were simply notes that needed to be filed and the 'receptionist' had just left them.

'What are these?' she asked the 'receptionist' who was on shift at that time.

'Those are people who haven't paid,' she replied casually.

'What do you mean, haven't paid?'

She shrugged and said, 'They haven't paid any money for their treatment.'

Jo added up the amount. It came to just over £1000 ($1600). She hit the roof and so did her blood pressure! She couldn't decide if it was the fact that no money had been collected or the blasé attitude towards this that made her so angry!

The second incident was actually two incidents involving one person. Again, it was a 'receptionist' at the centre of it. She asked to speak to us after a session in the centre. She wanted a raise in her salary. We pointed out that she had been given a raise two months before.

'You only have to see one more guest a day to cover it,' was her response.

Charming!

Soon after this, we discovered that money was missing from the till. Further investigation revealed that this same person was always on shift when it disappeared. We were so shocked by these events – first by the way the receptionist had spoken to us initially and secondly that she would steal from us too. We got ourselves in a terrible pickle about it. We couldn't understand how she could behave in such a way. We moaned about how ungrateful this person was. We had only good intentions towards all our team, we wanted what was best for them, and this was how we were treated. We were full of indignation and bitterness. On further inspection, we discovered that this same receptionist had been taking holiday and Tipp-Ex-ing out the dates afterwards to claim more holiday than she was entitled to. She was also compiling the rota so that she got to work all the middle shifts and her fellow team members had to do the earlies and lates. Our 'staff' management was out of control. We didn't know how to handle it. She was a good receptionist. We were so shocked she would behave like this. We asked each other how on earth we could keep her but, at the same time, how could we cope without her?

It really shook our world. Steve was ready to quit and Jo had no idea what to do next. It was a puzzle that seemed impossible to solve. We hadn't signed up for this!

Then something so profound happened that it changed everything. Something so simple yet so far reaching that we feel the effects of it to this very day.

At The Kitchen Table

It happened at the kitchen table!

We had decided to take the day off. We closed the practice, told our 'staff' to take a day's holiday and we went for a drive in the country. We had to get away. Get a fresh perspective and consider the future. We did a lot of talking that day. We walked by a lake, stopped for lunch at a pub and really began to wind down. On the way home we stopped at a grocery store and bought pasta, tomato sauce and a bottle of wine to have for dinner.

It was at that dinner on the kitchen table that Steve asked Jo what she wanted from the practice. What she really, really wanted. At first, Jo was so stuck in what she didn't want any more, that dreaming and imagining her ideal practice was almost impossible.

Then (after a couple of glasses of wine) she started to get into it. She became animated describing it. She used emotional words and gesticulated passionately while explaining what it would look like, feel like and smell like. How the team members would be. What they would wear. How they would behave. The atmosphere, energy and positivity. When she was done, we changed places and Steve described his dream practice. We really got into it.

'Wait,' Steve said. 'Let's write this all down.'

In a cupboard under the stairs, there was a wedge of A2 sized plain paper. We had picked it up at a seminar a month or two before, and still had the clutch of coloured felt tip pens that we were given at the same event. We laid the paper out on the kitchen table, took three pens each, and wrote all of the emotional, passionate 'doing words' or 'doing phrases' that described our dream practices. Just as we had described them to each other earlier. We did it fast and without editing. In the end we had about fifty of them. Fifty words that spoke of what we wanted, what made us passionate and what got us excited. From those fifty words we formed a statement that encapsulated all the things we wanted to say about our WOW! practice. That statement changed everything.

This process is now called the Keyword/Key phrase process. The statement that is formed from it is called, 'The Intention Statement'.

These first two simple steps were central to everything we achieved subsequently. From the Intention Statement, we formed all of the 'recipes' that became central to our WOW! practice model. It governed how we acted, how we spoke, what kind of energy we had, the number of guests we wanted to care for, how we would reach out to them, and how we presented ourselves in the healthcare industry. It led to our membership system, how it was managed, and the ethos and philosophy behind it; it helped form our relationship-chiropractic model that we teach all of our students. It even told us what the colour scheme of the practice would be, what would hang on the walls, what aroma would linger in the welcome area, what music the guests would hear when they arrived. It was the seed that began it all.

What Was The Result?

The results were dramatic. We went from being two practice owners living half in excitement and half in despair, with a group of mostly disengaged staff who relied on Jo to solve everything, who were lack lustre with low energy, on auto-pilot, slightly bored and who regularly went sick, to a team that was fired up with what we were going to achieve. They played full out to bring the new

Intention Statement to life every day of practice – to make it alive and tangible to all those who sought out our care.

Our relationship-chiropractic model meant we quickly acquired an army of guests who became raving fans and loved what we were doing. Our well-being membership system allowed our fans to be part of our practice. We had dinners together, we had summer barbecues together, cheese and wine parties. Their numbers swelled and swelled. We moved to a fourteen-roomed practice that we fitted out to reflect the Intention Statement completely. The colours were autumnal, the sound system played 'rat-pack' standards, we partnered with Starbucks coffee to bring a fully blown coffee house experience to our welcome area. We served latte, americano, mocha and iced coffee. The benches were luxurious, our adjusting rooms were spa-like, the walls were covered with textured wallpaper, the carpets were deep and rich.

We went from a standing start, an idea in our heads, to a WOW! practice with a million-pound turnover, through being ethical, honest and focusing on WOWing our guests and team. Of course, we appreciate that not everyone would want a million-pound practice, so before writing this book, we decided to re-test our recipes and our Intention and Culture, and created a smaller WOW! practice. This time around, we were not seeing guests ourselves and, through empowering some of our key players to use our success strategies, that practice went from another idea in our heads to a turnover of £250K in one year. It took vision, hard work, teamwork, and our strategies. So we know that these strategies work whether you want a big or smaller WOW! practice. One site or multiple. If we can do it, so can you!

One of the things we are most excited to share with you is our lifestyle membership. In monetary terms, we created two ethical practices with a turnover of well over £1 million ($1.7 million) per year, with a lifestyle membership alone having close to one thousand subscriptions. Each subscription was worth an average of £40 per month. That's £40,000 ($60,000) every month before our practice had even served our new guests and those who were experiencing their initial programmes of care with us. The financial abundance we created meant our team enjoyed the fruits of the collective hard work. In addition to a secure job (and extended family who cared about them loving their job), our practices were able to provide unique business opportunities for our management team, fun days out, spa trips, personal development opportunities, free chiropractic and life coaching, restaurant visits and trips to theme parks. One of our highlights was the day we gave our entire team a surprise bonus each, some receiving a cash gift and others the latest iPad, as a thank you for all their commitment to our Culture. (Please note I said their commitment to our Culture, NOT for their hard work generally.)

We also achieved our dream of taking our team on an all

expenses paid vacation to Las Vegas to attend the Parker seminar. We have had a ball and they are literally our second family. We have a framed picture of us with our team on the window ledge in our lounge at home! We love these guys.

Personally, we were able to create an exciting dream board and set about manifesting it, buying our dream house, sending our kids to private school, and paying for private health care for our loved ones. We took holidays in the most exotic places in the world. More important than the material things, we created opportunities for others; we were able to get involved with our favourite charities and community projects. Ultimately, we created financial freedom, a business we love and lifestyle choices.

Most importantly, through using our Intention and recipes, our teams were able to serve a whole army of guests who desperately needed what we had to offer. We gave people hope and helped when the medical profession had told them there was nothing that could be done. These guests have become our friends. Their friends and families have become our guests, and now they are our friends too. Our practice has had a transformational effect in so many ways and on so many lives.

We are so proud of what our WOW! practices have achieved. We are proud of our team – our second family – because they helped to build them. We are thrilled to have helped other chiropractors change their lives too. Now we are truly honoured to help you achieve your own WOW! practice and transform your life and that of everyone around you.

We don't tell you all this to impress you. We tell you because we believe you deserve this too! We know you can have it. We know you can handle it.

Ultimately we want to change the way you think – from an 'employee' mindset, someone who owns a job in a practice, into the mindset of a chiropractic business owner. This new way of thinking will transform the way chiropractic is practised globally, and help more people discover the amazing benefits of chiropractic through the interactions and care they receive from inspired chiropractic teams worldwide.

The Brave New World

We believe the traditional chiropractic practice is stuck in a model that is now outdated. In the old world, the practice is as good or as bad as the lead chiropractor. The lead chiropractor is almost always the owner. She sets the pace, sets the atmosphere and adjusts a very busy list of guests. She is in the practice all the time and guests love her. The staff rely on her to keep everyone on board, on side and enthused. She is the glue, the framework everything hangs from. Her energy, her drive, her personality push it forwards. The team waits to see what she does and then feeds off her. They do it again and again and again, just as she sets the energy and the pace and the atmosphere again and again and again. She sets the discipline; without her, the rules are bent out of shape. She picks the team up when they are feeling ill, down or personal problems are getting in the way of work. Not once or twice, but it's a never-ending requirement to do it over and over. The personality of the practice is hers. Her DNA is all over it. The 'nurturer/nurtured' relationship with both her guests and her staff is well established. It leads to a one-way street of energy that moves from her and is received by everyone else. Without her, the team 'make it up' depending on how they are *feeling*. When she isn't there, the 'life force' of the practice disappears.

We call this 'the dysfunctional chiropractic family' syndrome. It is dysfunctional because any relationship in which energy flows one way only is inherently out of balance and unsustainable. It leads to disillusioned, tired and ultimately burnt-out chiropractors who will throw in the towel and go and find something else to do if they are not rescued from it. Doing it the old way is very hard work. In fact it's exhausting. It can push even the best of chiropractic owners very close to the line of burn-out and breakdown. We attended a Gonstead seminar a few years ago where one of the speakers said that fifty per cent of graduate chiropractors will no longer be practising five years after graduation. If that is true, then this is a big part of the reason.

In the new world, the lead chiropractor *facilitates* the drive forwards. She is not solely *responsible* for it. The energy, the drive, the atmosphere and the pace are set by the practice's Intention. That is the thing responsible. Yes, the lead chiropractor is there to uphold it, to nurture it and to encourage the Intention. However, the new practice has an agenda of its own. The team is called to the Intention. They are motivated to drive the practice towards it whether the lead chiropractor is present that day or not. They might look to her for encouragement and guidance, but they are in no doubt what is required and they push the practice towards it at all times. The Intention builds a Culture. It is a Culture that builds the practice. The Culture attracts and retains dream team members and life long relationships with guests. A Culture that is strong, that is emotional, that speaks of something bigger than both the practice and the team, a Culture that is upheld and loved and nurtured and cared for, will prevail. The managers work with the Culture. They work on their personal and professional development within the *context* of the Culture. The team wants to learn and grow and come to work to be one hundred per cent present. This will build a WOW! practice for all who work as part of it, and a WOW! practice will build a dream life for the team and the owner.

Take it from us.

Practice Management Solutions

Practice management solution programmes are plentiful. In the early days of our chiropractic business journey, we tried many of them. They are often built on sound principles. The advice they give is valuable in many ways. There is a something for everyone. But by their nature they are 'one size fits all'. They are built around scripts and systems and ways of doing things.

Let's be clear, systems (or 'recipes' as we call them), scripts, and ways of working are vital. Absolutely central to the success of any practice. It doesn't matter if it's a chiropractic practice, a dental practice or a medical doctor's practice. However, scripts and systems alone are only as good as the person using them. The thing that these programmes leaves out is the intangibles. The central pillar, if you like, that they have never come to grips with; the thing that keeps guests returning time after time. Management systems do not teach the business owner how to create **Culture**. They teach him 'systems' that may well make him busier in terms of his list, but will lock him into the tyranny of doing his job over and over again, years into the future, just to maintain his practice at this new level. Culture and systems are not the same thing.

The central thing, the main draw of any practice, is its Culture. It's not its 'systems' or its high-tech x-ray equipment, the 'efficiency' of its staff, the 'professionalism' of the chiropractor or any of the dozens of other things that most chiropractors think it might be. Look at Starbucks Coffee Houses for instance. Why do people return time after time? Yes, the coffee is good (just as your chiropractic care has to be good), but they keep coming back for the intangibles. For the 'atmosphere', for the 'feelings', for the 'experience' they have while there. This is about Culture. In Starbucks' case it is about the deliberate creation of a Culture – a context – in which customers can experience drinking coffee.

The scenario we painted earlier of the burnt-out chiropractor is a culture too, albeit a destructive one. Management solution programmes do not teach Culture. They teach chiropractors how to get busier. To earn when *they* adjust more guests. In other words, they trap the chiropractor into (what we call) the employee/practice owner mind-space.

They do not teach the relationship-chiropractic model that is the most vital component of any business, especially a chiropractic business. Having a weak Culture, or a dysfunctional one, is like building a car without an engine. It looks great, everything on it works and is shiny, but it has no guts. No drive. No central locus of energy to push it forwards.

Implementing systems, teaching a chiropractor how to be busier in a *Culture-less* environment or, even worse, a Culture which is dictated by the strongest staff member (personality wise), is a dangerous exercise. The practice then becomes all about the system. It becomes mechanical. It becomes like a conveyor belt, and the system works only as far as the strongest staff member allows it to.

Recipes Bring Culture To Life!

In the *Crack It!* practice, *recipes* not systems bring the Culture to life. They push the practice towards its Intention. Towards the thing – that emotional, passionate, beautiful thing – that the chiropractic owner envisaged when she created the practice's Intention Statement. Recipes are the servant of the Culture, not the master. This important point cannot be overstated.

In the new world, chiropractic practices will offer a membership model that allows the chiropractic to be enjoyed within the context of the practice Culture. It allows an ongoing relationship with the practice and the team members (both clinical and front of house) who were so instrumental in moving the member towards their health aim. The membership model ultimately builds a relationship-centred approach to chiropractic that allows New World practices to flourish.

The Time For Change Is Now

Change is often difficult. It is scary. Moving from what we know, from what we understand (even if it is driving us nuts!) to something of which we have little or no knowledge, is one of the most difficult things we can do.

Change is also difficult for another reason. Perhaps for the most fundamental of all reasons – it takes a lot of hard work! Dedicated, concentrated, consistent work. At least in the beginning. It's like pushing a great boulder forwards. At the start it is all effort with little reward. In terms of a chiropractic practice, the amount of effort required to get the boulder moving will be directly linked to three important factors. They are:

1. The stage of development the practice has reached.
2. The number of team members (or staff) working there.
3. The determination of the chiropractic business owner to make the change.

Let us explain further by looking at the stages of a practice.

The beginning practice has a lot of energy; lots of frantic, excitable energy. To implement profound change (of the type we are advocating here) would be relatively easy. The momentum is there to do it. The vibe is positive and fresh. Team members are less likely to be 'stuck in their ways' and resistant to change. The *Crack It!* process is ideal for this type of practice. However, these very practices are the least likely to take any action at all. The reason is quite simple really: why should they?

They are feeling good. Actually they are feeling great! Really very, very happy. The owner has finally freed himself from his old associate job, and a boss who was 'opinionated' or 'ungrateful' or 'greedy', or any of the other adjectives that associates deem their old bosses to be! He is feeling alive, he is feeling FREE! At last he has done it. He is now master of his own destiny and can sail away into a sunset where things can only get better. Who can blame him? We've all been there, haven't we?

Few beginning practices look to the future. They do not look past the initial energy and drive to the mid-term. They never assess the challenges they might face up ahead (even if they do not yet understand them), and never decide to take action from the beginning. If they were to do so, they would avoid so much of the pain that comes with a practice built around little else but frantic energy.

The intermediate chiropractic business is a different animal. Often the practice is in pain (or at least the owner is). Not physical pain but mental and emotional pain. The practice is stuck on a relentless roller-coaster ride. Our 2003 business, which we described earlier, is so typical of an intermediate chiropractic practice. We don't need to labour the point here, except to say that the motivation to implement *Crack It!* principles is often great in these practices. But – and it is a big but – the price of doing so (in the owner's mind at least) is equally as great. It will mean changing so much. Altering the way the practice does what it does. Perhaps even changing what it stands for; how it presents itself; the recipes it uses to serve its community. There will be resistance from 'the staff', from the associate chiropractors, from just about everyone. They won't want to change. Why should they? They have it just as they like it, thank you very much. To drive change forwards, to keep it afloat, will need a lot of energy. Does the intermediate practice owner have that kind of energy? Does he have the will to do it? More to the point, does he believe – we mean *really* believe – that he *can* do it?

The answer to that question will dictate his future. However, one thing is for sure. If he does not believe it, if he does not implement it, the treadmill he has created for himself will go on turning and turning and turning.

The advanced practice is obsessed with growth. With expansion and influence. It wants to stretch its tentacles to touch more lives. It wants more of everything. But it is frustrated because it has not yet figured out how to do it. How to leverage it. The strategy that got the practice this far is no longer working. At least not for the next step. It is stuck in ways that were great for then but are not right for now. The appetite for change in these practices is usually good. The team members are less resistant to change than those in the intermediate practice, because they have had to adapt and change already in order for the practice to get to the advanced level. In most cases, a total overhaul is unnecessary, although it is sometimes needed if the practice is particularly ambitious. The biggest stumbling block to change in these practices is ego. The practice has a lot to be proud of. It has achieved good things doing it this way. But what next? How to take it to the next level? The owner of the advanced practice is often driven. Usually he is charismatic and intelligent. He knows he wants to move forwards. He *needs* to move forwards. He knows not doing so can mean stagnation. Boredom. Potential lapse and decay. He is not willing to accept that. Yet he is unsure how to go about it. Taking outside advice can be tough. What should he do?

The Challenge

So where do you and your practice fit in? Can you place yourself? If the answer is yes, then that is the first step in making a change. This book is the culmination of ten years of building our dream chiropractic business and helping other chiropractors build theirs too. We have experienced every conceivable challenge. They are the same challenges you face today. Chiropractic practice really can be an exciting journey. The highs and lows experienced in practice often mirror those experienced in life – and usually at the same time! This is no coincidence. All said and done, a chiropractic practice (or our guest list) is a true reflection of ourselves. The good bits and the not so good. The fears and the courage. It's all there waiting to teach us another lesson. A lesson about who we are.

Changing your life (and we've deliberately used that phrase here) takes a lot of effort. Those who are experts in change management tell us that the more you can perceive and imagine the benefits of that effort to change, the more energy you will put into it.

Over the years, we have attended workshops, seminars, coaching calls, and read thousands of books that helped us with both our chiropractic business and our personal lives. We have given seminars on how we built our practice, what the turning points were, what key steps we took, what our 'secret' was. In all those sessions we knew that only a few attendees would ever take action on what they had learned. Very few. Just the top one or two per cent. Most would devour the knowledge, revelling in what the future would hold should they model the strategies being taught. They might even spend a few half-hearted days attempting to put into practice the techniques they had learned. However, as soon as they hit a challenge, a difficulty they didn't envisage, they would go straight back to their old ways. They might tell everyone how profound, how life-changing the book or the seminar or the course was. Yet they would do little about it themselves.

What we are about to share with you in this book has not been discovered by reading or 'doing research' or thinking, or by being 'seminar junkies' or observing or understanding or philosophising. It is based on action. It is based on experience. It is based on honest, hard work and a relentless determination to get it right. We've done it. We've made mistakes, we've made superb decisions, we have had heartache and pain and we've had incredible highs and joy. We've beaten out a path so that you don't have to. Why reinvent the wheel?

And so the question is simple:

Are you ready?

Are you ready to truly change your life and your practice?

You are curious. That much is for sure. You wouldn't have got this far had you not been at least curious. But are you *really ready* for change?

And no, this is not some sales technique to get you pumped up before reading, or some 'salesy' psycho-babble designed to work on your subconscious.

It is a simple, honest, truthful enquiry into how you are feeling. You see, during the *Crack It!* process there will be challenging bits. Bits that you don't understand, bits you don't agree with, bits that make you irritated, bits you like, bits you love. Much of the work here will mean changing the way you think about your practice. We want to transform the way you perceive it. The way you approach it. That takes effort and commitment. You will have to fully engage with the process and take full responsibility for its success. You will, of course, have to implement it too.

So this is our challenge. If you're up for it, then we would like you to sign a pledge. A commitment, if you like, to implement the strategies we outline here.

Here's the pledge:

I am committed to achieving my dream life and my dream practice. I accept that it will take time and effort and I am absolutely prepared for that. I am also prepared to have my thinking, my belief systems, my ways of doing things challenged. I am fully prepared to step outside my comfort zone, leaving the safety and security of old thinking from time to time. I will throw myself into this book with vigour and treat myself kindly and compassionately throughout the process.

Signed: ______________________________

Date: ______________________________

Did you sign it?

If so, great.

If not, why not?

What's stopping you?

Go back and sign it. It's important. Then go on to the next section.

THE FIVE Vs

Whether you are imagining your dream practice for the first time or re-imagining your current practice and re-engaging with it, the process is the same. Building from scratch or deconstructing it to build it again, is a bit like building a house. When a builder builds a house, he uses plans. Architect's drawings. He first lays the foundation. Then he builds the structure. The structure is the meat of the house. He uses bricks and mortar and wood to do that. Finally he decorates the building. He designs a look for it. A lasting feel that the house will be known for.

The same is true with a chiropractic practice. We first need a set of plans, then to lay a solid foundation before building the structure; before bolting together the architecture. After we have done that – really done that – we can build and decorate. We can beautify it. We can add to it.

Similarly with the *Crack It!* process, it can be treated like building a house. There are five main steps involved in building, growing and maintaining a successful practice. We call them the **FIVE Vs** of practice design. This is the blueprint we used to build ours.

Here they are:

1. **Vibe**
2. **Velcro**
3. **Voyage**
4. **Visibility**
5. **Visceral**

That's it, just five. The rest of this book will be devoted to these and the ideas behind them.

1

VIBE

'I've learned that people will forget what you said, people will forget what you did, but people will never forget how you made them feel.'

MAYA ANGELO

The Vibe is a feeling. An emotion. It is felt by all those who work in your practice and all those who visit. It will give (or should give if it is created properly) a gut reaction. An intangible emotion that is real and convincing. The visitor should either like it or dislike it. Very few should be indifferent to it.

The Vibe should be felt on each and every visit.

The Vibe is made up of two concepts. The first is the **Intention** of the practice, the second is the **Culture** of the practice. Each of these two concepts is fundamental in creating a world-class practice.

Intention

The Intention of a practice is the central tenet of the Vibe. Every practice – in fact every business – needs an Intention. It comes before anything else and animates all areas of the practice. This is why it is the first and the most important step in the *Crack It!* process. An Intention – at least in the way we speak of it – is not a *vision,* nor is it a *purpose* or a *mission.* Business seminars often talk about these things. Trouble is most of us don't really understand what they mean and the difference between them. A few businesses have a mission statement. It has usually been 'knocked together' because the owner felt they ought to have one, and is tucked away in a drawer somewhere out of the way where no one can see it. The person who wrote it has either forgotten what he wrote or forgotten he wrote one at all. The rest of the team are not even aware the statement exists.

Mission and vision and purpose statements are confusing. That's why we do not advocate using them. The last thing anyone needs when setting a future course for their business is a confusing array of statements that the business has to live up to. For us there is only one thing required: one rallying definition of what the practice does, what it stands for, what it radiates, what it looks like, who works within it, and what it represents, and that is its **INTENTION STATEMENT.**

Our practice didn't have an Intention for the first two years, and we moved along in a roller-coaster ride of ups and downs. The practice relied on our energy, our personality, our soul, our desire to push it along. It was dependent on those things all of the time. Every day. Day in and day out. It was never ending. We realise now it was because we stood for nothing in particular. Yes, we wanted to do a great job – to be caring with our guests, to be energised and enthusiastic. We wanted our practice to be successful and those that worked with us to be happy. We wanted good things for ourselves, our team and, of course, our guests, but these were vague wants. They were not set in stone. They were not written down where we and everyone else could see exactly what we wanted and expected. They were not framed in a way that energised us, represented us (and our team) and fired us up.

When we consult with chiropractors (especially those in pain), one of the first things we ask them to do is explain the Intention for their practice. Almost none have any clear idea of what it is or should be. Therefore there is nothing tangible to unite the practice. Nothing that anyone in it (or indeed those who visit it) can rally to. No theme. No stance.

An Intention, if arrived at in the right way, will change all of that. It will give focus and energy to the practice. It will dictate what is acceptable and what is not. It will animate everything in it. If it is put at the very centre of the business, then the whole business of *doing* business – the decisions, the difficulties, the 'staff' issues, the angst of it – will be transformed. Questions will change from, 'What should I do in this or that circumstance?' to, 'Does this decision take me nearer or further away from the Intention?' The decisions that are taken – the only ones that are taken – should be those that move the practice towards the Intention.

There is a structured, well-defined process that leads to the creation of an Intention Statement. We call it the **Keyword/Key phrase** protocol. We take a whole day to go through the process in our *Crack It!* seminar series. It is not complicated, but it is important, and the protocol used to arrive at it is just as important.

There are a few fundamental points you should know about the Intention Statement. First, it should speak of the things that bring you joy. Things that get you excited. Stuff you love to do. Not necessarily 'business stuff' or 'work stuff', but the kind of things that speak to you emotionally. And speaking of emotion, most of the words you use in your Intention Statement should be emotive (to you at least). They should speak of your passion, your desire, your enthusiasm for what you want to achieve. These will not be wishy-washy words or phrases. They will be bold and confident. They will speak of heart and soul. When putting together your Intention Statement, it is very important that you steer clear of non-emotional words or sensible phrases or cerebral words. Here's an example of what we mean. Words like 'professional' or 'efficient' or 'comfortable' or 'tidy' or 'nice' or 'friendly' have no place in an Intention Statement. No place at all. They are sensible, cerebral words. So many chiropractors want their practice to represent these types of words. There's nothing wrong with these words per se, but not when you are creating a strong, definite Intention. Something that defines who you are, what you want and what brings you joy. We'd expect any practice – even the most ordinary practice – to be at least efficient and friendly and nice and so on. The rest of the world is doing ordinary. The rest of the world is great at doing nice, at efficient, at professional, at average.

Very few are doing outstanding or world-class.

The Intention Statement will not be overly long. One or two paragraphs is usually more than enough. It will be written in the present tense as though the things you aspire to, the goals you are determined to reach, have already happened. Oh, and this isn't an English test. The statement doesn't have to be a beautiful poem or a flowing section of prose! It just needs to come from your heart using the **Keyword/Key-phrase** protocol.

This is what we came up with for our practice in 2003:

> ***We are a dynamic and expanding Chiropractic Centre, committed to giving the highest quality of care by being***

consistently enthusiastic, efficient and dedicated to chiropractic. We care for and educate appreciative guests who want optimum health for themselves, their families and their friends. We offer lifetime care to all who seek our services.

If you study this statement, you will notice we have used the present tense and made it a statement of fact. No qualifying words, no half-hearted phrases, no ifs or buts, no excuses. This is how it is (or will be from now on). This is what we intend; not a version of it. This is not a reflection of what *most* of us in the practice want or what we *hope* to achieve. This is a statement of what *is*.

Also, notice the word *efficient* up there? What on earth were we thinking by putting *that* in? That should never have got through. Inexperience is our excuse. Suffice to say, it wouldn't appear if we were doing it today!

So let's recap on just a few reasons why an Intention Statement is so important:

- It gives the practice a stance. A stand. It is often said: 'If you don't stand for something, you'll stand for anything.' That is as true for a chiropractic practice as for anything else. The Intention sets the standard.
- It guides the practice – 'Is the decision moving the practice nearer the Intention or further away?'

- It provides a focal point. A flag around which all the team can gather.

- It prevents owner/chiropractor burn-out. The Intention sets the pace, the energy, the Vibe, the enthusiasm, *not* the owner. He is there to encourage and support. He is there to guide, to remind the team of the Intention and what it stands for, but he is *not* relied upon to drive things forward alone.

- It is a powerful entity in its own right that will call people to it and repel those who are not inspired by it. This is exactly what we want. We don't want to please 'all men'. We can't anyway. So we may as well stop trying to.

- It enforces the high ideals the practice owner envisaged even when he is not physically present. The Intention is a living, breathing thing. It watches over a practice like a benevolent father. It is central to every endeavour the practice takes on. We suggest you have it on view somewhere in the practice where everyone – including your guests – can see it. It should never be shut away. It should be in everyone's face all the time. At meetings, get togethers, huddles. It should be omnipresent.

- It leads to **Culture** and Culture is the second fundamental requirement for creating Vibe.

Culture

Whether you have one team member or twenty, you must develop your Culture. The term 'culture' is defined in the *Oxford English Dictionary* as *'the total of the inherited ideas, beliefs, values, and knowledge, which constitute the shared bases of social action'*. The Culture is the very thing that sets you apart from other businesses like yours. It forms the basis of the 'this is how we behave here, this is who we are and these are our standards'.

A clear Culture will attract like-minded people to your practice and repel those who should not be a part of it. When people walk into your practice – whether they are guests or potential team members – they should feel the Culture and know immediately whether they love or hate it.

Your Culture comes from the Intention Statement. The Intention is the standard that all behaviour in your practice is measured against. It is the standard that dictates energy, guest interactions, ways of acting, courteousness, attitude, positivity. It dictates values, social norms, teamwork and accountability. The list goes on and on. Let's explore this a bit further by using the Intention Statement we formed for our chiropractic practice in 2003:

> ***We are a dynamic and expanding Chiropractic Centre, committed to giving the highest quality of care by being consistently enthusiastic, efficient and dedicated to***

chiropractic. We care for and educate appreciative guests who want optimum health for themselves, their families and their friends. We offer lifetime care to all who seek our services.

Lets take the first 'emotional' word in the statement – *dynamic* – and explore how that word alone has helped shape our Culture. *Dynamic* to us meant a number of important things. It meant high energy, a 'can-do' attitude, positive, upbeat, happy, action-orientated. These qualities had to be demonstrated by our team members. The centre had to vibrate with that kind of energy. Not once or twice but all the time. It was part of the Intention and so we refused to compromise on it. But there was more to it than that. That word reached further and in unexpected ways.

Let's give you an example. Some of our most successful marketing campaigns are based on what we call 'personal appearances' (more of that later). Personal appearances (PAs) mean we go out into the community and introduce ourselves to those who badly need what we offer. It is great fun, it means we meet interesting members of our community and afterwards, the team members who 'appear' go out for dinner.

It became apparent (when we focused on our Intention) that those team members who were most in line with it – especially those whom we felt most *dynamic* – would invariably want to be part of the PA crew. They were fully displaying the high energy, can-do qualities that we were looking for. Other team members who were not quite as aligned rarely appeared. This led us to introduce a PA register. Simply put: we registered those who took part in PAs and those who did not. Therefore it became a measure – an objective measure – of those who were subscribing to the Culture, and ultimately the Intention, and those who were not. It then became an easy job to remind those who were not that the Culture does not allow for half-hearted subscribers. When faced with this truth, those who were not fully supportive left (with love) to find a Culture that they could fully subscribe to. That saved us so much heartache and stress. Everyone knew where they stood. It was not personal, it was all about the Culture.

We'll say it again: the Culture is derived from the Intention Statement. If you break down your Intention Statement into its 'emotional' word components, and ask yourself what those words really mean to you, you will have a powerful guide on how to set the Culture. So, *dynamic* is our first emotional word. Our second is *expanding*. Expanding is an interesting one. To us it meant a number of things. It meant that the practice had to be growing at all times. Expanding its reach. Changing more and more lives. Having an increased impact in the world. It also meant that our team members (including us) had to do the same. They had to grow and reach out, they had to push themselves to achieve more, break through barriers and limiting beliefs. They had to develop. They had to *expand*.

This word had a massive impact on our Culture. It led to our 'strat days' (more on this later), our self-development programmes, our sense of self. Our whole ethos changed. Our attitude to guests changed too. We wanted to expand their lives. To help them be the best they could be. We wanted transformation. That one word is responsible for so much of what makes our Culture unique.

A consulting client of ours recently told us (after a discussion about Culture), '… Looking at my current team, it is clear I need to change them all …' This is common. When a business is started it rarely has a strong Culture in place. As time goes on, the business will become a mishmash of individual wants and needs. The staff members are often unofficially led by the person with the strongest character, the strongest personality in the group. It is often his or her wants and needs that are satisfied (which are almost never in line with the business owner's wants).

Bear in mind that a good proportion of people look for jobs purely to earn money – they are looking for a place to 'survive' and 'wait out the day' until home time. They do their job, get paid and look forward to the Friday feeling, then dread the Monday feeling. These people have no place in your practice.

Our client complained about having to give energy to people working in her business who didn't want to work to her rules. She had found herself with a Culture of complainers who spoke about how hard they had to work and how busy they were. They called in sick a lot, took endless breaks and showed up late for work. They said no more than yes, when asked to help out other team members. We helped her create a Culture that reflected her deepest wants and desires, a positive place where people were happy and energised and followed her rules. As a result of changing this one thing, she kept just one member of her previous team. All the others left in the months that followed. This one remaining person was transformed by what had happened and became the new leader of a great new team. The process was tough in some ways as the business owner had to stick to her new business Intention. However, she didn't have to 'sack' anyone. When the complainers realised she meant business, they left. There was nothing to keep them there because they did not subscribe to her new Culture. They subscribed to the Culture *they* had created.

To 'stick to her guns' meant that this client had to have a lot of courage. **Ask yourself if you would have the courage to do what she did?**

Tough one isn't it?

You have the right to work alongside and lead passionate individuals who want to do the best job they can and are motivated to help your business be great. Your team deserves to work alongside a strong leader with high standards for themselves and their business in line with the business Intention. With a strong, positive Culture, the 'thank goodness it's Friday' people won't want to join you, and if they do accidentally get in, they won't hang around long. Imagine, rather than giving your energy to the negative people (and having to waste time trying to energise them), they leave rather than messing you about, calling in sick or moaning and bitching. The Culture encourages them to leave and you can let them go with love to become some other business owner's 'nightmare' – not yours!

Creating Your Culture

We have already established that the Culture is derived from the Intention. The Culture consists of a mixture of other things too – the standards, the business recipes, the community of team players. In our business, we have found it useful to use a metaphor for the Culture. It has been dubbed 'The Chelsea Bus' in our case. Everyone in our business knows and loves the Culture by that name. It was created at a time when the British football team, 'Chelsea', was winning all the top competitions and was the best in the Premier League. 'The Chelsea Bus' (TCB) is an imaginary bus which needs world-class players, and those who are passionate to learn how to be world-class, to sit in it.

During our job interviews, we talk to interviewees about our TCB and tell potential team members that in order to 'play in our team', they have to want to play in the best team. Not *be* the best necessarily, but *want* to be the best. There is a difference. We are not looking for 'superstars' to work in our practice (although some have become just that!), we are looking for those who *want* to be 'superstars'. Those who have that aspiration. In other words, we are looking for a 'superstar' attitude. Our team can fail as often as necessary. That is not important. It is *attitude* that is so vital. Their attitude must be in line with our Intention and our Culture.

Our team created a list of ten attributes that all of us in the team had to display in abundance. We called the list, **The Ten Tenets Of Culture (or the TT list for short)**.

These attributes were not job-related, but attitude-related. They set the rules of belonging to TCB. The true Culture-subscribers loved the Ten Tenets, while those who were half-hearted subscribers were challenged by them. That is exactly what we wanted.

The TT list sent a message to potential new team members (and existing ones) that if they wanted to play with our team, they had to be committed to being the best they could be and staying the best. If they knew they were not up for this, we invited them to go and work for another team in a different division where they may be more suited.

So our Culture developed and we added outstanding team players, and started attracting more and more people who purely wanted to play full out and be part of our TCB. Our team wanted to surround themselves with top-of-the-league players. Developing a strong, positive Culture of dynamic individuals meant that our staff turnover reduced and the right people stayed. Occasionally new people started, stayed a couple of months and left the bus. That was fine because rather than hang on in a place where they were not suited, they simply told us, 'It's time for me to get off the bus.' We could then work out the smoothest way for them to leave. Either they had lost their passion for our business and our Intention or they wanted an easier life. In most cases, we expected it was going to happen in their case anyway (the objective measurements of Culture subscription is a good indication!), so we either had the chance to rectify factors that may have wrongly influenced their decision to leave, or we simply had a chat, determined when they would leave and celebrated them with a lovely leaving do. Ending business relationships this way has meant we have been able to stay in touch positively with people who have left our team. Prior to our Culture, we wasted endless hours in disciplinary meetings, struggling to cope with poor employee behaviour and giving energy to the wrong people. This is common among new business owners: they spend their time and energy sorting out the not-so-great people and leave the great ones to become uninspired and un-coached.

Strategies For A Great Culture

It should be remembered that creating a great Culture and maintaining it is a team effort. The team members hold each other accountable for maintaining the Culture. Below is a selection of tools we have used to build and maintain our Culture:

1. A service agreement or contract

Every team member should read and sign a copy of their contract or service agreement. This sets out the 'terms' under which they can join and stay in the team.

2. A clear job description

This is the role that you want that person to play in your business. It avoids confusion and conflict as everyone is clear what they are expected to do as part of the team.

3. The pledge

Every team member signs a pledge each and every morning, which means that they will abide by the team standards.

4. Team room notice board

The team room should display your positive signs and affirmations that help the team stand united. Here is the place where all the promotional information is put so that everyone knows when the next personal appearance is and can volunteer (more about that later).

5. The team courtesy system

A system to ensure that team members love and respect each other as well as the guests.

6. The weekly coaching session

Every star player has a coach to help them reach their potential. Your star players are no exception. To reach his true golfing potential, Tiger Woods has a world-class coach to help keep him at his best. Your team needs your coaching. We hold weekly coaching for all team members on subjects that range from clinical management to outstanding guest care, through to communication and personal growth.

7. The monthly meet

We hold a monthly meeting. It is compulsory for every team member to attend. It is a condition for staying on our bus. At this meeting everyone has a voice. We have a suggestion box for ideas about how we can improve the business. We vote a team member of the month (they win £30 in vouchers) and give feedback on how the business is doing. We discuss our targets, our aspirations and even our frustrations. It allows every team member to be involved and feel part of something bigger than themselves.

8. The huddle

At the start and end of every shift we have a team huddle. The purpose of this is to reaffirm what we want to achieve as a team during that shift, set the Intention for the shift and check that all the team are passionate advocates for the business. Then at the end, we feedback two positive things and one not so positive that have happened during the shift. We immediately suggest ways we can improve on the next shift. Each team member takes a turn to join in. Everyone starts and ends their working day feeling great.

9. Birthday system

We celebrate each person's birthday with a gift and card from everyone. Every team member contributes £1 for each person in the business on a yearly basis. Celebrating birthdays helps to boost team morale and, if our team feel great about themselves and each other, they will also feel great about looking after our guests.

10. Captain's Log

Every week we have a Captain's Log, normally written by a senior member of the team. The log re-centres us and gives us one area of the business to think about. In addition, each team member sends feedback to the log-writer, in which they recognise at least one team member who has upheld our Culture in a WOW! way that particular week. It is a process of reaffirming the positive Culture, capturing people doing great things and recognising them for it, rather than concentrating on negatives. Everyone loves to hear great feedback about themselves! It is a very popular email that goes out every Friday at 6pm. Oh, one interesting point on the Captain's Log – when a team member consistently does not add any comments about their team to the log, it is normally a sign that they are either not thinking about all the great things that are happening within the team, or that their passion for the Culture is waning. Therefore we always measure who is logging without having to be reminded and who isn't!

11. The Strategy days

Four times a year, we close the business for two days. The first day and a half we spend working on ourselves and on the business, on our growth and expansion, on its growth and expansion (expanding is one of the 'emotional words' in our Intention Statement, remember), and we work on our skills and goals for the business. For the last half of the second day, we go off and take part in a team building activity. Over the years we've done all sorts of things. We've all been to a spa, we have tackled an army assault course, been zoo keepers, fire-walked over hot coals, done board breaking to overcome limiting beliefs, climbed high ropes, played the 'Apprentice' game, we have shot rifles, run, crawled and climbed (blindfolded!), and relaxed and laughed and cried. All as a team. These activity days are always high-energy and action-packed. We often see huge team breakthroughs during the Strategy days. Team morale and support are paramount.

12. Team captain access

The leader should make themselves available to their team regularly so that any team members can pop in for a chat should they wish to.

13. Reporting support chain

Each section in the team needs a leader, so we have leaders for our clinical team – one for our chiropractors and one for our massage therapists. We also have a separate leader for our front of house team. If our team members (or our guests) have a challenge, they know who they can go to to get it resolved.

14. Buddy system

When someone new joins our team they are paired up with a buddy. This is the person who helps them settle in and ensures they are welcomed into our Culture. This is especially important for graduates who have often relocated from a different part of the country to join us. The buddies meet regularly to discuss their goals, their hopes, their dreams. They keep each other on track, inspired and loved. Most importantly, they keep each other aligned with the Culture.

15. The holiday/absence system

When a team member cannot be present at the practice, it is their responsibility to find another team member to cover them. Our goal is that 'our show must go on', and we all take this very seriously.

16. The monthly social

We run a monthly social, which is normally a meal or a few drinks, and all the team are invited to join. It helps to bond the group and gives people the chance to socialise with other team members they may never normally get to see outside the centre.

17. Personal development library

We have a personal development library that has books and DVDs team members can borrow in their quest to grow and expand. If someone buys a book they think will go well in our library, they give us their receipt, we reimburse them for their book and add it to the collection.

18. Chiropractic and personal development seminars

Throughout the year we take our team on chiropractic and personal development seminars. Even though we believe we are great chiropractic mentors, our team thrives on hearing positive chiropractic messages from someone else.

19. The guest newsletter

Each month we release a guest newsletter with a gossip column in which team members can add pictures or stories about what they have been up to. Our guests love it when they hear about someone running the marathon, see wedding pictures, read baby announcements and so on. We used to pour lots of energy into a more formal newsletter but we discovered something interesting. Guests are much more interested in the *relationship* they have with our centre than anything else. Let us explain. The response to one of our early newsletters was much greater than to any other we had produced up to that time. The reason? It included a photograph of our wedding in Las Vegas. It was the first time we had included anything like that, and more guests commented than ever before. Nowadays most of our newsletters are centred around our chiropractic family and what they are up to. Very little of the content is about purely chiropractic.

20. A team goal

Set goals as a team and celebrate when you reach them. We once set a goal that resulted in an all expenses paid trip to Las Vegas for the whole team! This was a very large goal of course, but smaller goals can be great fun too.

Maintaining The Culture

As we said earlier, whilst it is your job to ensure all team members are playing in the right team, it is up to the team to maintain the standards and Intention. When someone falls short, any team member can support them and help them back to being the best they can be. Equally, if someone is not playing the game and creating issues or challenges, the team can nudge them gently to get them back on track. Not allowing mediocrity into the team is a team effort!

A strong, loving Culture creates an empowering environment; a supportive, encouraging setting for all those who subscribe to it. If you get it right, be prepared for other people – those outside your business – to call your business a 'cult'. That is exactly the reaction you are after! It is a 'cult' after all – it's a 'cult-ure'! You know you are doing something great if your Culture gets described that way. A cult of positive people who want to be the best they can be. How amazing!

WAKE UP CALL

- To achieve your WOW! practice you must have a strong and clear Intention and Culture.
- Your Culture should exist with or without you physically present in your practice.
- Your life outside your business should reflect your Intention and Culture within it.
- If your Culture is all about *your* energy you will very likely burn out.
- Be like 'Marmite' – people should either love your practice or hate it.

ACTION POINT

Do you have an Intention for your practice?

If you do, write it here:

If you don't, then write some keywords to get you started:

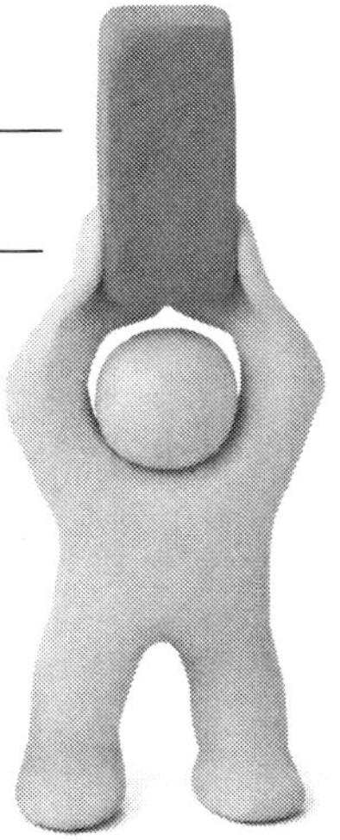

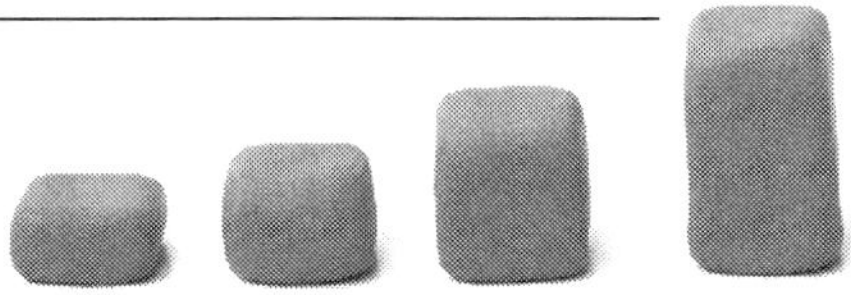

2

VELCRO

'Individually we are one drop, together we are an ocean.'

RYUNOSUKE SATORO

'How do I attract really good people to work in my practice?'

That is a question we hear all the time. The chiropractor asking it will usually follow it up with: 'And how do I keep them when I do?' This is where your practice's 'stickability' comes in; its ability to act like Velcro on both team members and guests. If you have read this far, you will immediately grasp that a large part of your practice's Velcro-like quality can be found in the Vibe. The Intention and the Culture. Team members old and new are attracted to what they *feel* when in your practice. Do they feel excited? Energised? Empowered? Or do they feel uninspired or daunted? They will be attracted to it or they will be repelled by it. Either is fine as long as the reaction is strong.

Those who are in line with what you have created will stick like Velcro. Those who are not will pull away. But that will only happen if you stand for something. Something bigger than the practice. Bigger than you and everyone in it.

But what else should be considered? The first thing to remember is the difference between staff and team. Staff are the individuals you pay to come and be physically present in your practice. They carry out a job that they are paid to do. Your team is a group of people who work together to achieve a common goal in line with the Intention of your business.

Team:

T: Together

E: Everyone

A: Achieves

M: More

So banish the word 'staff' from your vocabulary and your business right now! Your team members are your 'crew'. They are the people you put together to represent you and your business Intention. Let's say that again: your team represents you! So be sure that these people are worthy of representing you.

Attitude

The number one thing you are looking for from a great team member is a great attitude. You can teach systems, dress code and chiropractic philosophy but you can never teach someone to have a great attitude. We would much rather have an inexperienced, fresh person with a great attitude, than someone who is experienced with a bad attitude.

One of our best team members started with us as a work experience kid. However, she stayed on afterwards and became one of our 'Saturday Team'. If you asked her to do anything, she always replied, 'Of course I can.' She was eager, cheerful and one of the brightest, most diligent team members we have ever had the pleasure of employing – yet she was under eighteen years old. You deserve 'of course I can' team members!

The Captain Versus The Boss

In our vocabulary, the boss and the captain are two different animals. Hopefully the next section will demonstrate why we make the distinction.

Before you start recruiting your WOW! team, you need to work on being a WOW! captain. The captain is the person ultimately responsible for the business being a success. The team works alongside the captain to achieve a united outcome; reaching the goals initially set by the captain. As the team grows, it becomes part of the shared Intention. The team members are there to commit to the project and to their captain, and are in alignment with the business Culture. Staff, on the other hand, are a group of individuals paid to do a job by the boss. They have no real vested interest in the project or its outcome. They do their job, put in their contracted hours and get paid for doing so.

We were once asked to give some coaching to a CA from a very successful chiropractic practice. The practice manager told us that the lady was very keen at the start and now seemed to have lost her 'mojo'. The owner wanted to discover what had gone wrong. Was she a bad hire or had she got lost along the way?

We sat with the CA and asked her to tell us about her role. She lit up and went into a lengthy explanation of how much she loved caring for the guests and educating them about chiropractic. She loved being part of chiropractic. But when we asked her about her captain, her persona completely changed. She started to cry and explain how the female owner came in every day and didn't even say 'good morning'. She described how she walked past her and straight into her room. The CA felt let down; isolated. She felt the captain was always looking for the things she hadn't done correctly, and never mentioned all the good things she had done. She said she felt criticised and undervalued. To add to the frustration, the boss's husband would call numerous times throughout the day to speak to the boss and, when she got off the phone, the boss was always grumpy and even more off key. The CA expressed how difficult it was to be happy and polite and upbeat, while the boss wasn't. She started crying even louder when said, 'She doesn't even know my name – she calls me Lynda, yet my proper name is Lydia. I haven't said anything as it's been going on for months ...'

We explained that the captain was relatively new and so she didn't have all the answers, and told the CA she should speak to her directly. She agreed to do so. Days later, we heard from the captain. She told us that the CA had gone to speak to her but (in her words), 'she got all emotional and gave in her notice'.

This is an example of the need to act like a great captain and not as a boss before adding team members to the practice. If we treat people as staff, they act like staff. After discussing this episode with the practice owner, it became clear that she was frustrated with this CA. She felt she had hired the wrong person; that her energy and style of work was not suited to the practice. The captain had begun acting the way she did as she didn't know how to move her on and get someone more suitable.

However, by reviewing her Intention and revamping the recruitment process to meet that Intention, she now has the CA of her dreams. She is much happier, the new CA is happy, and the guests are too. They have fun at work! As a result profitability has also increased. The change was in the captain, not in anyone else. She was not acting like a captain at all, she was acting like a boss. And a poor one at that. She had not made it clear to this CA what she wanted and expected. The CA had no strong Intention to follow, so she floundered. The captain's frustration boiled over and it ended in tears (literally). These days she has a clear Intention and is creating a strong Culture. Everyone in her practice knows where she (and they) stand. There is no confusion now. That is the sign of a good captain.

Your team is a reflection of you. If you are going to be leading a great team, you need to become a great captain. A team cannot flourish unless the team captain is determined to become a great leader. The most common reason people leave a business is because of their boss. She is too aggressive, too demanding, indecisive, rude, grumpy. A bad boss can never attract and retain great people.

A captain plays a similar role to the one he plays in a sports team. A captain trains and plays to the highest standards. He brings the team together and works at keeping them focused on the Intention. He has to adhere to the same rules as the team. He does not have a separate set of rules from everyone else.

Secrets Of Being A WOW! Team Captain

If you want to become a WOW! captain there are a few basic principles you have to follow. The previous example of the upset CA illustrates the need for the captain to know the Intention of her business and to set the Culture from it, so that all team members know where each stands. Every captain must know at least that much. But there are other strategies too. We teach these to all our coaching clients (and, of course, to our own group of captains). They are:

1. Develop a positive outlook and lead from the front

Don't expect your team to do tasks that you are not prepared to do yourself. One of our junior associates once remarked to Jo, 'I get it. To be successful I need to become a clone of you.' It was said quite innocently. And, yes, she did have to 'clone' Jo if she wanted to achieve the same success. If she wanted a different success, she would need to find a different successful person to 'clone'. As Tony Robbins says, 'Find someone who is doing what you really want to do and model them.'

Whilst we want our team members to think for themselves, it is much easier to coach and lead someone who wants to have the same standards as you do. Remember, if you arrive in the morning positive and raring to go, this will infect your team positively. If you turn up and grunt at them and then disappear into your own world, don't be surprised if your team turns into a group of 'grunters'. When you then ask them to be welcoming and polite to your practice guests, they will become confused as your own behaviour is in conflict with the behaviour you want them to display. Your team will start complaining about double standards. As team captain, when you arrive in your practice, greet each team member by name, make eye contact and smile. Touch base with them and ensure they are happy, healthy and well.

2. Choose your team wisely

Every member of your team represents you! They are not doing you a favour by being on your bus. Use a profile system that ensures the person you appoint has the correct skill set for the job. If you are looking for someone to work in the back office, they do not necessarily need great people skills but they do need great attention-to-detail skills. If that same person was appointed by you to work on your front desk and give great customer care, then forget it! We will talk much more about recruiting later in the chapter. One of the first things we advise is using a personality profile tool on yourself and your team. We recommend a simple D.I.S.C profile. The great thing about this is that, once you have profiled yourself and discovered your work style, you are better able to choose your team and communicate with them more effectively.

When we first started in practice, we looked to recruit GP receptionists as we thought they would be a fit for us. However, we soon realised that they were about as far away from our ethos as it was possible to get! We wanted to offer an outstanding level of care, while they were used to the 'gate-keeper' mentality that stops guests getting in. Have you ever experienced a GP receptionist who asks you what the problem is? You want to talk to the doctor, not disclose your symptoms to a stern front desk receptionist to secure the appointment. This was not what we wanted for our practice! We only discovered the truth after they had been with us for a few months.

We have had numerous chiropractic coaching clients who have told us, 'My reception staff are good, so I will train them as we go along and slowly introduce them to chiropractic.' Good luck! Your recruitment process should select those with a skill set for the job; an appetite to know everything they can about chiropractic (and a strong desire to enjoy chiropractic care). Then (and only then) should they be trained in 'your way of doing things' – before they start. This will cause you much less hassle as they progress. Starting your team members 'on stage' from day one isn't a strategy for success. Spend time teaching them behind the scenes first. Then unleash them into the Culture.

Other clients have told us that they have 'receptionists' who have never experienced chiropractic. We believe that everyone in your practice must be a positive advocate for chiropractic. They are the people helping educate your guests about chiropractic. If a guest calls up and asks your front of house team about chiropractic, especially about the adjustment, what message does it give if your receptionist says, 'I have never had one so I don't know'?

3. Treat people as if they have already become what they are capable of becoming

You have a dynamic team, not a herd of sheep. Your rules need to be clear. Then once people know the rules, you need to let them play. Great players love to be coached but when they are playing they love to shine. If you don't let your players shine, they become frustrated and leave to shine elsewhere.

Strive to let the team solve its own problems. Being firm and fair means that all the team members have the same standards and expectations. When we started in practice, and we didn't have any systems or recipes in place, we lived under the constant strain of not knowing what our front of house team was saying and doing. We were in our rooms adjusting, hoping they were taking care of guests in the way we wanted. However, the team had no idea what that meant. We remember once being on holiday and calling them every couple of hours, panicking about what they were up to. Hire someone to carry out a role, teach them the role, then treat them as if they are the expert in the role and watch them fly.

4. Letting go

All right, so it is your baby and you created it. However, your business must survive without you. If it is all about you, you are on your way to a breakdown and the team you will attract will be sheep. Trust us, we have been there. Back in 2003, we were in a place where every waking moment we were thinking about the business. Putting in a strong Intention, a strong Culture, then backing it up with congruent recipes and allowing dynamic people to think and use their skills to implement them, was a huge factor in allowing us to grow.

5. Be respectful

To gain respect, give respect. Simple. We have already explained the importance of a courtesy system. We recommend all businesses implement at least this. Shouting at your team, no matter what they have done, is never the best way to empower them or encourage them to be better. Just as you want your team to be respectful to you, be respectful towards them. Giving respect garners respect. If you need to have a chat with a team member, do it backstage. Never reprimand someone in front of others. If you have to reprimand someone for not doing something they should have done, tell them clearly and non-emotionally, reset the standard, give them the chance to shine and provide positive feedback afterwards. This motivates the team. Telling them off and not allowing them to shine just makes them resentful and you frustrated.

6. They will find me out

Many team captains live in fear that their team will 'find them out'. They worry that their team will discover they are not the guru who has all the answers, and this can stop them from recruiting great people. They look for people who are not as good as they are, rather than focusing on recruiting people who have different skills to their own and unleashing them into the business to do great things. Celebrate yourself for who you are. Don't worry about the things you are not.

7. Keep working on growing yourself

A big part of being a successful team captain is continual self-improvement. We have spent thousands of pounds developing ourselves, adding to our own business expertise and working on our own personal development. Most great leaders invest in themselves. It is vital.

8. You become like who you 'hang out with'

Great team captains need to surround themselves with other

great people who want to be the best they can be. They buddy up with other business owners or those interested in personal development, and join (or set up) accountability groups that help them stay on track. If you hang out with people who have never owned a business and discuss your business and your life decisions with them, you will get bad business advice. Good-intentioned but bad advice. They are people who have different goals and standards for themselves. Do not do it!

There is a group of people in life – we call them the two per centers – who are truly committed to being the best they can be. If you consider the wider population, ninety-eight per cent of them are not committed to anything other than getting through their day so they can go home and do something more interesting. The two per centers are those who are getting on with doing the things that the ninety-eight per cent say cannot be done. Hang out with two per centers. These people will inspire you to continue to grow, and help you be the best you can be. You can find people like this by joining groups such as the 'Yes' group or the myriad of Facebook mastermind groups. Or you could create your own!

If you find yourself only hanging out with people who work 'for' you, the advice they give and the place they are coming from means that you cannot be who you really want to be. A client of ours once told us, 'I own a business that employs forty people and I can't talk to any of them.' He meant he couldn't talk to any of them about things that truly mattered to him. Of course he couldn't. How could they understand his business challenges, his worries and his fears? They had never been in business. They didn't know what it felt like. They had never 'put skin in the game' as an American friend of ours once called it. They had never felt the responsibility of paying team members, covering the lease, the overheads. Of keeping it all afloat.

So choose who you hang out with wisely.

9. Get a coach

All serious athletes, professional sports players and great business owners do not expect to get to the top of their game alone. They all have at least one world-class coach alongside them, guiding them, pulling out the best from them. All great team captains must follow this strategy. The coach's job is not to tell the captain what to do necessarily. Instead their job is to help the captain stay focused on the business Intention and assist the captain to stay on course. They are a bit like a sat-nav. You tell them your destination and they help find the best way to get there.

10. A mentor

A business mentor is someone who has already achieved your goal. Get one!

The Multiple Hats Of A Great Team Captain

As team captain of your business, you have to wear a multitude of hats. When your practice grows your management team will do the same. The challenge comes when you try to wear all the hats at once. Let's consider a chiropractic business owner. Many are trying to do all the roles in their business, often all at once, which is a road to burn-out. We teach our clients to imagine they are team captain of a world-class sports team. At times they need to play in the game, at other times they coach the team. They need to know the rules too, because they have to umpire on occasions. In chiropractic terms, playing in the game means they are focused on seeing their guests. Whether it be seeing new guests or adjusting them, they have to be fully present and focused only on the guest. Coaching is the separate time they give to their team to help them be the best they can be. Umpiring is the time they spend doing behind-the-scenes business tasks.

Most chiropractic business owners wear multiple hats, but they do it *at the same time*. We did that too. We had not been in practice long when a particular day dawned. We had a list full of guests but the cleaner had not turned up. So we quickly cleaned the toilets and ran the hoover around before our guests arrived. At the same time, we were involved in a front desk issue – someone had called in sick at the last minute – and another staff member (they were staff then) informed us that they couldn't come in and cover. It also happened to be bill-paying day and so, in between guests, the finance lady came to get us to sign cheques. In addition, our associate had a 'difficult' guest and had called upon Jo to come in and help with that too. Then there was another team member who needed to have a chat with Steve about a personal issue. Trouble was, Steve was organising a promotion. Halfway through the day, we were completely exhausted, and still had to lead the monthly meeting at lunchtime before heading back in to see guests in the afternoon.

We quickly learned that, in order to stay sane, we had to develop the ability to wear different hats at different times. So the player/coach/umpire metaphor helped us and our team to manage time better (ours and theirs).

So to recap:

PLAYER – This is the hat you wear when seeing your own guest list or helping the associates during their list.

COACH – This is the hat you wear when you are coaching and supporting members of your team (you must not allow yourself to wear this hat when you are seeing your own guests).

UMPIRE – This hat is for when there are no guests and you need to do jobs relating to the running of the practice. Anything back stage. Paperwork, bills, marketing etc. You cannot see any guests or do any coaching during the time you are wearing the umpire hat.

Once your team members understand your different hats, they know when you are available to coach or help them. It makes everything clearer and allows you to balance your role as a business owner, chiropractor, leader and team captain.

When you are seeing your guests, you must be fully present with each guest and not thinking about finance worries, bill-paying, team issues or who has called in sick. Being all things to all men and at the beck and call of your team whenever they need you is the road to ruin. The open door policy should exist when you are wearing your coaching hat. During this time you should be fully present and ready to serve.

When To Recruit

A chiropractic business owner should recognise when it is a great time to recruit and when it is not.

Only add team members when:

1. Your systems are working and you have time to support, coach and nurture the new team member.
2. Your business is about to go through a growth cycle.

Do not add team members when:

1. You need a day off.
2. You feel burnt-out.
3. Your business is losing money and you want help to make it more successful.

The act of recruiting a new team member means you are prepared to invest time, energy and money supporting and coaching them. Clients who have been about to recruit have often said the dreaded words, 'That new person is going to be great. They want to be busy and I can leave them to it.'

The new associate (who has often just graduated from college) will require coaching, a mountain of positive input clinically and emotionally, and you will spend a not inconsiderable amount of money and time on the process. They will waste and 'mis-manage' many new guests during the initial periods as they will have no idea how to 'manage' their guest lists. Do not take this lightly.

Newbie Or Not Newbie?

We prefer to recruit newly qualified chiropractors. The reason is simply because we prefer to work with people who have not developed bad habits working for someone else.

Remember: successful recruiting is a process. Here's a step by step guide to the way WOW! practices do it:

1. The advert

Place an advert at the colleges and with your association approximately five months before chiropractors are about to graduate. Do not mention hours or salary.

2. Observation

Unlike traditional interviews, never simply meet the candidate. Ask them to adjust you and then offer them a job. You are about to invite someone to join your chiropractic family. So it needs to be a similar process to finding a life partner. When someone responds to your advert, arrange a time when they can come and meet you. Ideally they should come and observe you in practice for a few hours. Being with someone in your room will allow you to see their energy, their initiative, and how they interact with your guests and other team members.

3. Send them away

Once they have observed you for a couple of hours, take ten minutes to chat to them purely about what they are looking for. Note their comments. Tell them about your Culture and Intention. Then advise them to go and see as many other practices as they can and, if they are still interested in working with you after that, they should come back. Some people worry that if they say this, they will lose the associate to another practice. Personally speaking, there has never been anyone who was right for our practices who went somewhere else. If the person was a potential two per center, the more practices they went to see, the more they wanted to work with us. Reason? Those practices were busy being 'efficient' and 'professional' and 'friendly' and 'nice'. They were in the ninety-eight per cent. If the associate chiropractor is in alignment with you and your Intention, she will have had this reinforced by going and seeing other practices. If she would rather be in another practice then that is great as it saves you employing someone who just wanted any job. The best candidates will naturally go and look around anyway and will be more drawn to you if you are not desperately offering them a job on the first meeting.

4. The second observation

When they return, ask them why they wanted to come back and who they have been to see. Then you can talk to them about your practice Intention and the type of role you are offering. Tell them about the role, the coaching and apprenticeship process.

5. The associate position

Only take associates who want a full-time position with you. You do not want an associate chiropractor who works somewhere else as well. This will dilute your Intention and make it much harder for your associate to be successful in your practice. Full-time commitment is what you need to really help this associate become the best they can be.

6. Pay

This is a biggy! Gone are the days when you should be paying your associate fifty per cent when they arrive with you, even though this may be what they will be expecting (and what they have been told at college). Trust us – when an associate starts with you, he or she might be clinically competent. However, they will not know how to attract guests, manage guests and educate them in the way your practice requires. If you want them to work in line with your Intention, to be an asset to your practice, you will spend vast amounts of time (and money) coaching and helping them. They will mis-manage many of your guests and lose them to your practice. It will cost you, your practice and its reputation in the short term. This is mitigated by your constant input, your time, your effort, your energy, your service to that young graduate.

We measured (in 2011) how much money employing a graduate costs our practice in the first year of their time with us. It makes for interesting reading. We estimated that, in terms of time we devote to a graduate's training, he will take around 390 hours in year one. If we assume that a chiropractor's income is around £120 per hour, that works out at £47,000 per annum. Then add to this the cost of guest 'mis-management' (meaning weak recommendations and guest education) in that first year, which will cost the practice somewhere in the region of £36,000. We therefore look to invest around £83,000 in the first year. On top of that, we (the owners) have the responsibility of the practice, ensuring it runs smoothly, it pays its bills, it grows, it soars. Why then would any chiropractic business owner offer to pay an associate fifty per cent or forty per cent of what they earn? It's madness – particularly as it is worth noting that the average chiropractic practice has an overhead of between forty and sixty per cent. One does not have to be a skilled mathematician to see our point ...

We recommend a tiered 'salary' system:

- Junior
- Intermediate
- Senior
- Managing

The better they do, the more they learn and the more they earn. We are going to commit to teaching them everything we know about clinical practice and running a successful business (they would pay a small fortune if they got an external coach to do this), so we take our 'coaching fee' from income from their guest list. The best associates have the opportunity to learn from a motivated team captain, and learn and earn more than they could ever have dreamed of in the future by employing our teachings, either in our business or their own.

We are clear about our associate programme. You need to be too! Have a structure which means the associate is nurtured, loved, supported, taught and empowered. Do not leave your associate isolated in a room, without a mentoring plan, paying them fifty per cent. It is this type of boss who results in the high number of disillusioned chiropractors leaving the profession.

We believe the most important role of the chiropractic business owner is to support their associates, giving them a great education in becoming busy, successful chiropractors, and teaching them to run successful practices. Giving them this and paying them fifty per cent would be a ludicrous business decision.

One of our clients once told us their associate had left after telling him he was taking too much of *her* money! A few months later, we discovered that the same associate was looking for someone to be her mentor for free as she felt isolated in practice! Sometimes associates want it both ways. They completely miss (because they are not in business) the time and costs involved in coaching.

Another client said to us, 'Do you ever get frustrated giving all the input when, after a few years, they may leave you to go and do it on their own?' Our answer was simple: 'No!' We have been coaches to them, we want them to be successful, we have given them the best foundation they can possibly have. We have received the financial coaching fee to support them and, if they choose to leave, that is fine. We are not losing them from our lives forever. Many remain part of our second family, and we are there to support them whenever they need us.

As a final note here, in case you are stressing about the amount of time and energy (and money) needed to devote to a WOW! associate, let us reassure you that the reward in terms of professional satisfaction is great. Remember, you are looking to build a mutually beneficial relationship.

7. Ongoing coaching

Our advice is for the team captain to set aside a weekly slot where he meets with his associate and assesses their goals, discusses cases and teaches them 'next level' stuff. We have special sessions – what we call 'obs and tech' sessions – where the associate is in the practice but not seeing guests. They start by just watching a more experienced chiropractor. They help the chiropractor; they take his clinical notes; they listen to how he speaks to his guests, how he builds trust, how he empowers them and how he takes them on a journey to lifestyle chiropractic. Once they have started to master their list and it has begun to get busy, we commence the process of teaching them how to move on to the next stage of the WOW! process. This takes them through clinical mastery, personal growth, the psychology of success and, penultimately, leads them to a managing chiropractic position before preparing them either to invest in our business or leave to set up their own practice.

These principles will help ensure the Velcro works well in your business.

Recruiting Massage Therapists

The same process should exist when recruiting massage therapists into your team. When we first set up in practice, a fellow business owner advised us not to bring massage therapists into the team. His rationale was that the guests would pick either chiropractic or massage and not have both. This was never our experience. When they are educated well, our members understand that it is chiropractic that has solved their problem and maintained their health, while massage – chiropractic massage – is an intrinsic part of the chiropractic journey.

We often get asked by chiropractors about whether they should add a massage therapist to their team. We love working with massage therapists. However, there is an important fact you must know before you do this. Many chiropractors add massage therapists to their team, leave them to work on their own giving their type of massage without chiropractic guidance, and pay them far too much. Whilst some massage therapists have university degrees in subjects like sports science, one can actually qualify as a massage therapist in a matter of months. They may be able to give a good massage, but often they are taught only basic anatomy and physiology. They have no idea how to educate their guests and how massage ties in with your style of chiropractic. If you pay them fifty per cent of their list, you find you are left without any profit and a whole load of hassle. Use the same recruitment process as with your chiropractic associates, and have an apprenticeship for them. We have worked with many massage therapists over the years very successfully by having them as part of our clinical team. We have also interviewed hundreds who were looking to hire a room or be on the fringe of our business. In the early days, we took on an MT to do a couple of shifts a week with us. We paid her fifty per cent. However, she had other 'fish to fry' as she was working in other places so didn't want to be part of our team, wanted different rules and didn't want any part in the marketing of the project. This meant that, whilst all the other team members were at promotions and taking part in educating our guests, she was nowhere to be seen. Equally, she wasn't fully integrated into our coaching programme. In other words she was disengaged from our Culture and our Intention. This was no good for her, for us and, more importantly, for our guests.

We were recently asked about this and the chiropractor client said, 'The massage therapist would normally charge £25.00 at home and so this is what we are competing with.' Jo nearly exploded in frustration as he was about to fall into the MT trap. As a chiropractor, only add massage therapists to your team if you want them working alongside you, they are passionate to learn about chiropractic and to become fully-fledged members of your clinical team. They may get paid more on an hourly rate working at home; however, at home they do not get to work alongside you – a great chiropractor who is referring guests to them! Do not underestimate how many fantastic massage therapists would rather work with you using the tiered payment scale, in line with what we advocate for DCs, than at home where they are on their own.

Remember, in a WOW! practice, the MT works under the chiropractor's guidance. He or she massages according to the instructions the chiropractor gives. There should be open and frequent communication between them – weekly meetings, for instance – to discuss each guest on the massage list. The guest/chiropractor/MT relationship is a triangle that should not be broken. If the MT leaves, the chiropractic massage guest stays in the practice. Chiropractic massage when combined with pure chiropractic can be very powerful. But all involved – guest, chiropractor and MT – need to understand that it is controlled by the chiropractor and is not an adjunct therapy that is somehow separate. Adding a massage therapist purely to come and give their style of massage to your guests will not add much benefit to your care programme, and it will add little profit to your business. In this circumstance, it is also likely to be a very one-way relationship, where you refer to them but they do not make it their business to refer new people to your practice. Rather than having the hassle, you might as well set up a reciprocal relationship with your local MT outside your practice and be done with it. Your guest will end up with the same experience of non-chiropractic massage anyway, yet you won't have the bother. As you can see, we feel strongly about adding great MTs to your clinical team under your guidance and terms.

Your MT team can be self-employed. However, the therapists must agree to become part of your clinical team and go through the same coaching and processes as the chiropractors. They must also sign up to your cultural tenets. We have had the privilege of working alongside some great MTs, as well as meeting many who would never be right for us, and vice versa.

The Front Of House Team

Chiropractic assistants (CAs) support the chiropractor in giving an outstanding chiropractic experience to each of the guests.

Receptionists are people who answer the phone, make appointments, take payments and are (hopefully) efficient. You need to surround yourself with chiropractic advocates at your front of house. They are people who are willing to learn and become passionate about supporting guests and members on their chiropractic journey. They have chiropractic themselves, their family has chiropractic, they love educating people about chiropractic. They would never call themselves receptionists.

We have met hundreds of CAs and hundreds of receptionists at our CA bootcamp seminars. On the whole, most are great. However, some chiropractic business owners need to go back to the drawing board and re-imagine what they want the front of house team to act and look like. Some seem to think that the receptionist is doing them a favour by coming in and sitting at their front desk all day.

CA Meeting And Coaching

Just like any team member, your front of house team needs regular coaching and meetings to help them stay on track and have a positive voice in your practice. Our CAs have weekly meetings with our DCs. They also have weekly meetings with each other and their team leader. They have 'clinical confidence' sessions too. These sessions are led by a DC and take the CAs through a case. Here they learn history, differential diagnosis, x-ray interpretation. CAs love these sessions. It allows them to see what is going on 'behind the curtain'.

What To Do If All Goes Wrong

Even with your strong Culture, sometimes 'intruders' slip through the recruitment net and you'll find yourself with the situation where you may have a 'misfit' amongst the group. The great thing about having a strong team Culture is that, on the whole, the Culture will persuade the intruders to leave. Intruders don't subscribe to the Culture wholeheartedly. That means they get rather miffed when others in the group (who do subscribe) start to hold them accountable. For example, one of the non-negotiable tenets of our Culture (we have ten) is the Captain's Log (as previously mentioned on pages 59-60). The Captain's Log is a weekly event where one of our captains will write an email to the whole group giving updates of what is happening in the practices: events, birthdays, celebrations. It will usually have a theme. Communication, for example. Lastly, every team member is asked to write a couple of lines mentioning one or two of their team-mates who have gone above and beyond to produce a WOW! experience for our guests. Contribution to this log used to be on a volunteer basis. It is no longer. It is compulsory. If a team member subscribes to the Culture, a few lines a week praising one of their team-mates is no hassle at all. For those who don't, it is a pain in the neck. We never ever advocate harassment and bullying of anyone in your employment. If you have someone who clearly isn't right for the Culture, keep reinforcing your message. Where there isn't alignment with your Intention, encourage them to go and find another Culture that they are in alignment with. With a strong vice captain and positive advocates for your business, their positivity means that the misfit's negativity will have no place to grow and infect your business. The challenge with misfits comes when the team captain or leaders have allowed a dilution of the Culture. In this environment, the negativity virus can become very infective indeed.

We once had a rather intense coaching session with a husband and wife team. They sat in our office and told us they were being terrorised by their 'staff'. The wife was in tears, crying that they couldn't make their business work after years of hard graft and input. The husband was a great chiropractor but had become disengaged from his team and was not upholding the Intention (which is not surprising because he didn't have one) and, as a result, the strongest personality in their practice was now taking charge. They had allowed a Culture to develop in which their associates had the weekends off while they (both of them) were in working. On top of that, they would organise and attend all the personal appearances (spinal screens, for example). The associates had no role in bringing new guests into the practice.

The business owners' challenge was that their associates had been allowed to behave in a way that suited them. As a result, our clients were left with a practice where they had all the stress and worry, as well as doing the hard work, while the associates did pretty much as they pleased. We set about coaching them, but when we said they would have to change some of their team, the wife became even more hysterical.

'We can't afford to change our team!' she wailed.

'Why not?' we asked.

'Because we'll have to start all over again!' she said.

Quite often it simply takes the removal of the 'strongest negative influence' and your team is happily restored to your Culture. But often you are faced with the difficult situation of removing a strong character who is popular amongst the group. They are popular because they are providing unofficial leadership, albeit leadership in a negative way. However, in the absence of official leadership, any leader will do. Fail to get them out and your life is headed for a whole lot of frustration and worry. In the words of Apple creator, Steve Jobs, 'It is better to have a hole, than an arse-hole!'

One of our clients who recently started with us made changes very quickly and had a great team, but also had one MT who caused stress. This lady was a magnet for any negative feelings, negative energy and negative team members. She would gather it all around her. As a result, she always resisted joining in the activities that maintained the Culture. She didn't want to join in the practice promotions, she rarely emailed positive feedback for our client's Captain's Log, and she generally acted like a naughty school girl, doing the bare minimum and getting by. She wanted all the benefits of working in our client's amazing centre, but also wanted just to turn up, massage and go home.

We advised our client to meet with the MT (which he did), and explain that he was behind her one hundred per cent and thought she was a great massage therapist (which he did). However, to stay as part of his team, she needed to take the Culture more seriously. He listed the tasks she needed to carry out (which were the same as the rest of the group), and gave her a time-frame in which she had to do them. The MT was very pleased that he had taken the time to meet with her, and also felt encouraged by his support of her work. A few months later, she has ended up being a leading light in his team.

The converse of this example can also be true. In that case, the MT would have moved on.

So, please ensure you move 'intruders' on. Act fast, and let them go with love. Even if it leaves you short for a while, your team will rally around and deal with it. In fact they are usually delighted you have sorted it out and more than happy to help. Never compromise your business, Culture and yourself by forgetting that it is your business and your Intention, and that you are responsible for ensuring your particular dent on the universe is a magical one.

You deserve team members who are passionate about your practice Intention and want to strive to be the best they can be as part of your project. Anyone who doesn't want this is very welcome to go and join another project. Last note here: never worry about not being able to find someone to replace a team member. The nature of a highly dynamic environment means that there is always someone who wants to step up. Create the hole and the universe will fill it every time.

WAKE UP CALL

- You own the business. Everyone who works in it is representing you.
- You deserve the best!
- Do not compromise yourself or your business for people who should not be on your 'bus'.
- Never be scared to lose the wrong people. The great ones will always step up and help until more advocates arrive.
- There is always another great person just around the corner looking for you.
- Create a vacuum and the universe will fill it.
- Great team members deserve a great captain. They will not stay or shine with a 'bad boss' regardless of what you pay them.

ACTION POINT

Imagine your ideal team members. They are going to represent you and your practice. Describe them (male/female, older, younger, attitude, are they under chiropractic care?):

Think of an occasion when you acted like a captain and another when you acted like a bad boss:

List three occasions when you have compromised what you wanted for your business to placate staff, patients or family:

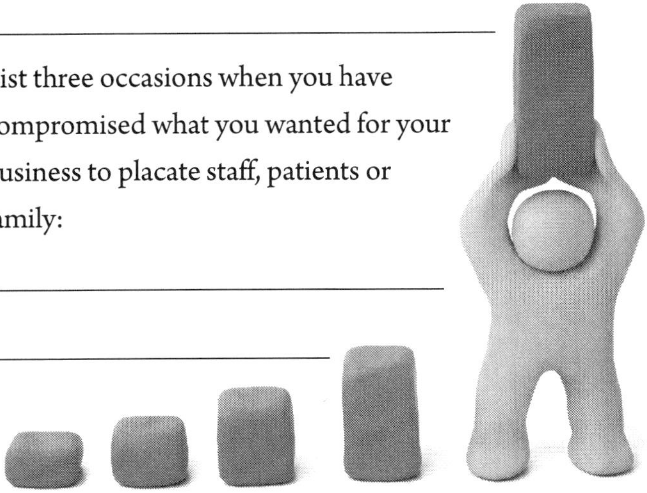

3

VOYAGE

'Every day is a journey, and the journey itself is home.'

MATSUO BASHO

The Voyage component of the five-step *Crack It!* process describes the journey a new guest will make within your practice. Every guest will go on some sort of voyage. A voyage from pain to wellbeing for instance, or from a sedentary lifestyle to an active one. The Voyage we are referring to here, however, is not about health per se, it is one of interaction. Interaction with your business. Interaction with your Culture and your Intention. Each guest must feel the full force of it at every stage of the Voyage. So the Voyage dictates what happens to each guest. But when does it happen and how does it happen? That is a question that needs a great deal of thought and will depend on a number of factors, including your philosophy, your Intention and your

Culture. The truth is, most chiropractors give this concept very little thought. When we ask them to describe a guest's Voyage through their practice, they are vague and unclear about it. They make general stabs but are rarely fluent in its nuances.

So let's set out three rules that define what the guest's Voyage is:

1. A step by step process that takes the guest from their first contact with you to their last.

2. The process must be clear, precise and repeatable.

3. You should be able to draw the Voyage out in a flow chart.

Don't confuse marketing with the Voyage, by the way. This is a mistake a lot of our clients make in the beginning. There is a big difference. Marketing your practice is the business of getting potential new guests into your practice. The Voyage is what happens when they are there. The Voyage brings together every element of practice. It combines front of house, clinical and administration.

The Voyage can be thought of as a funnel. The funnel is wide at the top and narrows at the bottom. At the very bottom is a plug with a few holes in it. The funnel is divided into sections which we call phases. There are four phases in a guest's Voyage. We refer to them as VP1 (Voyage Phase 1), VP2, VP3, VP4.

VP1

VP1 occurs *after* the guest makes contact with your business but *before* they enter your practice physically. They may approach you at a personal appearance, or phone in after being recommended by a friend, or they may check out your website after seeing one of your promotions. That first contact is all about VP1.

VP1 has two components. Both of them answer the two main questions a potential new guest has in his mind at that early stage.

The first question: 'Is this person/are these people experts in my condition?'

The second question: 'Can I trust them with my health care?'

The second question is much more important than the first and therefore it is imperative that you answer it.

These two questions should be addressed everywhere the new guest turns. Whether he speaks to you at a personal appearance, whether he browses your website, googles you or lifts the telephone to call your front desk. The first question largely addresses your ability to convey your clinical expertise to him in a *way he understands*. Giving a potential new guest a detailed lecture on his particular condition is rarely a successful road to take. He needs to understand what his problems are in layman's terms. Having said all that, he also needs to know that you could give him a detailed lecture *if* you so wished. So your initial interactions with him should certainly answer the first question.

The second question – the trust question – is something that will take a bit more time. Business analysts tell us that a potential customer will take around four 'touches' with your business before he feels he can trust you enough to pay for your services. These touches are even more crucial in the healthcare business where trust is such an integral part of the healing process.

Going back to our funnel, we do not recommend that you offer your product (your chiropractic services) to the potential new guest until VP2. By that time, *Crack It!* strategies ensure the guest has had up to ten touches with your chiropractic practice. At VP1 we aim to generate up to five touches with the potential new guest. The touches are all about trust. About who you are and what you stand for. They are about connection. About exposing the potential new guest to your Culture, to your Intention and values. This gives him space in which to make up his mind on the very important second question.

So our question to you is: can your potential new guest trust you with his healthcare? If the answer is yes, then demonstrate it to him. Connect with him frequently at VP1.

VP2

VP2 is the part of the funnel in which the potential new guest interacts with your practice physically for the first time. VP2 has two parts to it. VP2-1 (new patient consultation) and VP2-2 (report of findings appointment). At VP2-1, the questions a potential new guest has are no different from those he had at VP1. At VP2-2, they get a bit more extensive. Remember, the interactions at this stage are all about your expertise and whether you are trustworthy or not. Your job is to fully expose the new guest to your Culture, to the Vibe, to the *feeling*. Guests will rarely make the decision on whether to trust you based on logic. It is almost always an emotional decision.

Ensuring your guests have a great chiropractic experience at VP2 is a team effort. A DC may be excellent, but if his team is grumpy or scruffy or disengaged, the experience can never be WOW! Everyone involved in the guest's experience must be an advocate for chiropractic and for your practice. They should be advocates for the Culture and Intention too. They help create the Vibe. It goes without saying that they should have experienced a new guest examination with you and be having regular chiropractic care.

Quality control is a big part of VP2 and is often overlooked by practice owners and their team. However, a WOW! practice needs to be clean and tidy at all times, so there should be a good quality control system in place. You never get a second chance to make a first impression, as the saying goes. This is so true at VP2. The advantage of VP2 is that the potential new guest is physically in your practice. They can see, hear, smell and even taste your practice. They will have (or should have) an emotional reaction to it. They are making so many judgements about you, your team, your practice, your Vibe; whether they can trust you or not, what level of expertise you have. They are *perceiving* so much at VP2.

We explain this to our consulting clients using the analogy of a cup. Imagine a cup. It is delicate china, with a gold rim and dainty, bright coloured flowers hand-painted on it. How much would you pay for such a cup? Well, it depends from where you are buying it. If you were buying it in Harrods, it may have a price tag of £100. It will come packaged beautifully and you will take it away in one of their famous green bags. If you were buying it in Tesco or Walmart, it may have a price tag of £10. If you saw the same cup at your local car-boot sale, you would probably pay around 50p. It is the same product. Yet you perceive its value to be different depending on the setting in which it is offered. If your setting (your practice, your decor, your Vibe, your Culture, your Intention) is boot-sale standard, the value (and the trust) the potential new guest will place on your chiropractic services will be of that order. If it is Harrods standard, the value will reflect that too.

We would bet that the chiropractic care you provide in your centre – the skill, the art, the clinical competence – is at least equal to most other chiropractors in your area. But if your *Intention* is different, your *Culture* is different. Your *attention to detail* is different. In other words, if the *context* in which your chiropractic care is delivered is quite different from anything else, it has a whole new meaning to your potential new guest. The buying experience in Harrods is completely different to that of Tesco. You feel different. You feel special. That's the feeling you want your guests to enjoy.

So set your price in line with your Intention. People are much happier to pay for your services if you create outstanding guest-centred care. The least your welcome area should have is the following:

1. Robust chairs (no ripped material or wobbly legs).
2. Clean carpet or floor.
3. A clutter-free front desk.
4. Lights that are dust-free and in good working order.
5. Guest story books (a simple folder containing other guests' testimonials and pictures).
6. Chiropractic literature and leaflets.

7. Your registration certificates.
8. Kids' area (with photos or drawings done by young practice members).
9. An outstanding chiropractic advocate ready to greet and care for guests.
10. Smart décor.
11. A talking point – ours is Starbucks. Yours might be a huge tank of Koi carp, or a golden harp in the centre of the welcome area, or a picture wall – anything that speaks of your joy!

If you give your guests a third space, a place in which to relax during their time with you, they are much more likely to form a relationship with your Culture and your Intention. Their chiropractic experience will be more joyful. If they see it as simply a place to sit in when they wait to see the chiropractor, both they and your business miss out. The practice appeals to their logic only. Logic says, when they are out of pain, they will leave. So in our case, we created a welcome area that we dubbed (after the Starbucks tradition) the third space; a place where guests can have some time out from their busy lives, have a drink and relax. We call it our 'tea and coffee' Culture. Guests bring their friends in to experience our welcome area and almost always the friend becomes a new guest with us. If you have a drab welcome area and if you allow drab 'staff' to work in it, you will attract drab guests who only stay until their pain has gone and never get the full benefit of lifestyle chiropractic.

VP2-1

So now to the appointments. As you might imagine, we have recipes for every stage of the guest's journey. We recommend that you do too. Our recipes are designed to ensure that each and every guest receives, as a minimum, world-class chiropractic care. Care that is honest, ethical and life-changing. Care that is delivered within the context of our Culture. A loving, supportive, third space environment.

The new guest appointment with the chiropractor has three distinct parts:

1. The opening
2. Clinical concentration
3. The close – 'forming a triangle'

The aim of these three elements is to answer the two burning questions the new guest has. Remember them?

'Is this person an expert in my condition?' and *'Can I trust this practice with my healthcare?'*

The opening part of the consultation should allow the new guest to 'get everything off his chest'. To talk himself out. To unburden himself.

The 'clinical concentration' part of the appointment allows the chiropractor to do his job: to ask pertinent questions, to conduct a thorough chiropractic exam and to make some clinical decisions. In other words, to expose the new guest to his clinical expertise.

The close and 'forming a triangle' is designed to cement the next part of the guest's Voyage.

We realised many years ago that the 'transitional' stages of the guest's Voyage were often fraught with difficulties for both the practitioner and the guest. Frustration on the part of the practitioner if the guest did not move smoothly from one phase to the next; disengagement from the guest if they did not fully understand the part of the Voyage they were currently on and what the next part entailed. The triangle takes advantage of a phenomenon we discovered almost by accident. It is this simple fact. Human beings take much more notice of someone saying things *about* them than *to* them. The 'triangles' we form in our practice are designed to utilise this fact. Therefore they have become vital in moving a guest smoothly from one part of his Voyage to the next.

The Day Of The New Guest Appointment

Being prepared is the key. Prior to your new guest arriving, the CA should prepare a new guest pack and have the intention to WOW! them on arrival.

The new guest room should be checked to ensure it is:

1. Clean.
2. Smells fresh.
3. Has the correct equipment in it.
4. The carpet is clean.
5. The music is turned off (we have music piped to every room).
6. It is warm enough, but not too warm.
7. There is a chair for both the guest and the DC.
8. A clean, fresh smelling gown is available.

These may sound like little details. However, they are important in creating a WOW! first impression. The CA is like the personal assistant to the DC. If the room is ready in advance, the DC can concentrate on the guest rather than wasting time trying to prepare the room and locate equipment. Your CA will need to be fully present, energetic and passionate so that everything is ready for you and you have a smooth transition into the consultation.

The New Guest's Arrival In The Welcome Area

There is nothing worse than a new guest arriving in your practice and being ignored by your team. Consider how the new guest may be feeling:

1. In pain?
2. Sceptical?
3. Scared?
4. Anxious?

So the outstanding CA always looks out for the new guest and is ready to give them a warm greeting. A WOW! greeting is one that takes place within seconds of them walking into the practice. In other words, never leave new guests standing there waiting to be greeted. The greeting should include the following:

- A smile.
- The CA coming out from behind the desk and welcoming the new guest as if welcoming them into her house.

- Shaking the guest's hand.
- The CA introducing herself by name and welcoming the guest to the centre.
- The CA having a dynamic energy.

The CA never leaves the new guest. She sits next to them and will offer to fill in the answers to the questions on the new guest form or, if preferred, makes the new guest a drink while they do it themselves.

After the guest has completed their details, the CA should orientate the new guest to the practice. We suggest a quick practice 'tour' to help familiarise them with their new surroundings. Show them the adjusting area, the x-ray suite, the massage suite, the rehab room, the toilet. The WOW! CA will look for the guest's reaction – are they happy, scared, relaxed, questioning? Then, once the new guest is settled, the CA can offer them the chiropractic story book (more on this later) for the chiropractor the guest is about to see.

It is now the task of the WOW! CA to ensure that the new guest gets to see their chiropractor at the allocated time. If the DC is running late and keeps a new guest waiting, immediately the guest's perception of the practice is lowered. They are now experiencing similar treatment to the one their GP delivers. If there is a problem that cannot be avoided and the DC is going to see the guest later than scheduled, it is vital that the CA informs the guest.

VP2-2

This part of the Voyage defines the follow-up to the new guest appointment, universally known as 'The Report of Findings' appointment.

The questions a guest typically has at VP2-2 are more extensive than at VP1 and VP2-1. It is important to be aware of what they are. The guest will still have the two questions from the earlier part of their Voyage – the expertise and trust questions – but there are more now. The additional questions are:

- Does the chiropractor know what is wrong with me?
- Can it be fixed?
- How much will it cost?
- How long will it take to get me well?

The Report of Findings consultation must address all of these needs. The session should not include complicated jargon, it should not be an anatomy lesson, neither should it confuse or unduly frighten. It should explain your findings simply, succinctly and honestly. It should give your guest a realistic expectation of what she can expect in your practice. It should give a prognosis, a time-frame, and finally what investment of time and money the guest will be expected to make in order to reach their health aim.

The guest should be made aware at the start of her chiropractic care programme of the nature of the Voyage she is about to embark upon. The three stages of care, for instance: the pain stage – where the chiropractic team is mostly interested in relieving the symptoms. The 'rebuild your back' stage where the team is looking to improve function, and the third and final stage (lifestyle chiropractic we call it), where the guest enjoys optimum spinal health. The time and the cost involved to take your guest to their health aim should not be skirted around. Phrases such as, *'Let's see how it goes ...', 'I'll give it a go ...', 'It might work ...'* have no place in a Report of Findings appointment. They instill confidence in no one. Neither the guest nor the chiropractor. They almost always end with the guest failing to reach his health aim, the chiropractor feeling dispirited and the guest telling his friends: *'Chiropractic didn't work for me ...'*

There is a level of chiropractic for everyone. This is not a one size fits all process. If your practice Intention includes taking your guests from pain to lifestyle chiropractic, then you must have a proactive set of recipes that will ensure each of your guests receives the full force of your Intention.

VP3

VP3 is all about the course of chiropractic care the guest enjoys in your practice. It is the 'middle bit' of the funnel. The bit in which the guest's Voyage really begins to take off. During VP3, your guest will be exposed to the full range of your clinical and personal skills; your Intention and your Culture.

As mentioned earlier, we recommend that the Voyage is divided into three separate stages: the initial pain relief stage, a 'rebuild your back' stage, and 'lifestyle chiropractic'. The first two are not new to most chiropractors, but the third phase (at least the way we do it) is.

There are two main challenges the chiropractor must overcome at VP3. They are:

- Moving the guest smoothly between one phase of care and the next.
- Referring the guest out of the practice if he does not meet certain 'milestones' on the road to health.

Getting the second challenge right is more important than the first. Let's give you a quick example of what we mean by this. One of our chiropractors recently had a guest who repeatedly complained about the pain she was experiencing in her shoulder. She actually presented with low back pain but, since starting on her chiropractic journey, she had developed shoulder pain (even though the low back pain had now gone). The DC explained that this was a common biomechanical compensation and that there was no need for alarm. One day the guest was in so much pain that she was crying violently in the DC's room. The DC was trained in our systems and so knew when to refer out and how to do it. The guest told our chiropractor that the next GP appointment she could get was a whole week away. So the DC called the local private GP, booked an appointment for the guest, paid for it over the phone, spoke to the GP personally and also wrote and faxed a letter to the private GP. She then asked her CA to print out a map of the GP's address, told the guest to go and see the GP, and come back and talk to her the next day. When the guest arrived the following day, she was a different person. She was so overcome at what the chiropractor had done. The GP had been great and had been supportive of the chiropractic care she had been receiving. He administered some painkillers and gave her lots of reassurance. The guest was calmer and the DC was able to concentrate on adjusting her and helping her body heal. The guest only needed the painkillers for two days. After this, she became a raving fan of the practice and a frequent referrer.

Often it is not the amazing chiropractic care we give that compels guests to refer their friends and family, but the *loving* care the team shows. In this case, if the DC had not taken action, the guest would have ended up sacking the DC and going to a GP anyway. The cost of the private GP appointment was paid by the practice. However, this fee has come back hundreds of times over by the guest's referrals.

VP4

VP4 is the subject of the fifth and final step of the *Crack It!* process, and for good reason. We call it 'lifestyle chiropractic'. You might refer to it as maintenance or on-going care. Our experience with most chiropractors has shown that this part of their funnel is the least understood and is given the least amount of time and energy by the practice. One reason is that the practice is busy caring for 'new guests' at VP1 through VP3. The practice is distracted. It has 'other fish to fry'. The chiropractor is focused on the VP1-3s too. Guests at VP4 can often feel they are being taken for granted. Or they may perceive the level of care they are receiving has slipped. Either way, they are likely to leave your practice at this point. They almost always leave for an emotional reason, not a logical one.

It might seem a bit 'new age', but we teach all of our clients to remember this one thing at VP4. It is another question that the guest has. It is the main question at VP4:

'Does this person/does this practice still love me?'

That is what they are asking themselves all the time at VP4. If they *feel* you do not, they will leave to find someone who does. Or worse, they will discontinue chiropractic care and wait until they are in pain again. That is why there is a plug at the bottom of the funnel with holes in it.

Many practices not only have holes in their plug, but giant great craters! In step number 5 we discuss VP4 fully.

The Recipe Book

The Voyage step of the *Crack It!* process is the best place to highlight how important a 'recipe book' is to your business. The recipe book is a written proclamation of how you do things – how your Culture is maintained, exactly how you recruit new team members, how you train them, how you take a guest on a healing journey. The recipe book – just like a cook book – lists everything needed to create your business cake. Imagine that you want to bake a beautiful chocolate fudge cake. You ask your friend to make it whilst you do another task. Your friend follows every step of the recipe, but just as you are about to 'tuck in' to the creation, your friend realises they have forgotten to add the chocolate into the mix. You have a cake, and it may actually taste 'ok', but it certainly won't be the gorgeous chocolate experience you're expecting! Ultimately you're disappointed. Your practice is exactly the same.

Your practice is a business and, as a business, it needs to achieve its Intention consistently. We have already said that chiropractic business owners set up on their own to find relief. Relief from their old boss. Their old life. Working for someone else. When they worked as an associate, they attended work and then left to forget about it completely until it was time to work again. They didn't have to think about it too hard. As a business owner, you will need to think about recipes very hard indeed. Recipes that reflect the Culture for your business. We recommend you have a recipe for every aspect of the business; for every interaction; for every experience you want your guests to enjoy. We divide them into three:

- Front of house
- Clinical
- Back stage

Imagine your business to be like a West End show. It has a cast. Each cast member has a role to ensure the 'show' is a success. If one of the cast is absent, someone else can step in and the show is equally as successful. Much of our stress in the early days was because we had to do a lot of the practice running ourselves, balancing being clinicians with being business owners and bosses (not captains!). If someone left suddenly or called in sick, it put a huge strain on the rest of the team. Thinking of it as a show took a lot of the emotion out of it, as we were not worried about individuals who were indispensable. Don't get us wrong, we loved every single member of our 'cast'. However, the show did not *rely* on them individually.

The show had a back stage and a front of house. The front of house was visible to guests. Back stage was not. Our chiropractors and massage therapists were on stage, so was the front of house team. They were supported by a back stage team who carried out HR, administration, finances, compliance and so forth.

Rather than recruiting actors to fill these roles, we recruited people who were naturally in alignment with our Intention. When it came to caring for our guests, those we recruited genuinely wanted to care for them. So our cast members were playing the best version of themselves, not being false versions of someone else. If the role needs a cheery person, employ a cheery person. They love to play this role without any persuasion.

Examples Of Front Of House Duties That Need Recipes

Below are some of the functions at our front desk that we have recipes for:

- How to answer the telephone.
- How to book a new guest.

- How to greet a new guest.
- How to make an appointment.
- How to book a schedule of appointments.
- How to reschedule an appointment.
- How to open up the centre.
- How to take payment.
- How to process a guest on our computer.
- How to give a receipt.
- How to cash up.
- How to welcome a guest to the centre.
- How to make a drink ...

... You name it, we have it!

The goal is to ensure that every front of house team member plays their role as a positive, happy advocate for our centre. Each new team member is coached in our recipes. We do not employ robots. We recruit well so that people with great personalities, who are in alignment naturally with our Intention, use our recipes.

NB: watch out for the mediocre staff member who will happily tell you, 'I don't need recipes, I know how to answer the phone.' What they are saying is, 'Leave me to answer the phone my way, thank you. I don't need you interfering and holding me accountable to the way you want it done.' It is these 'staff' members who build empires in your business and prevent you from taking it to the next level. So watch out!

Creating Your Recipes

The purpose of your recipes is to achieve the Intention for your business. They are step by step guides that you and your team use to ensure your guests get a consistently great experience. This is never more important than at the Voyage step of the *Crack It!* process. Unfortunately, many chiropractors tell us they haven't got time to write recipes as they are too busy adjusting or dealing with issues within the practice. However, although time-consuming at first, once written and learnt and acted upon, your recipes will take your business and your life to new heights. If you have multiple practices, it is almost guaranteed that the one with you in it is the more/most successful and profitable. This is because 'your way of doing it' has not been formalised properly in the 'other' practice(s). It hasn't been taught to your team. It hasn't been drummed into them. They haven't been tested on it.

This is why 'other' (satellite) practices are typically nightmare experiences for the chiropractic business owner. They are full of team members 'making it up', and full of frustration for the business owner who ends up with too much hassle, too much stress and too little profit to sustain it all long term.

Here's what to do when creating a recipe.

First, be aware of the purpose of the recipe:

1. To ensure your practice Intention is achieved. We don't just mean a back office manual, we mean a recipe for every task – clinical and non-clinical – that takes place in your practice, from opening up, to making tea, to greeting guests, to administering care.

2. To ensure your guests get a consistently WOW! experience that is bigger than the personality of your CA who happens to be on the shift at any given time.

3. To create certainty for the business owner.

4. To make it easy for team members to master their roles and be successful doing them.

5. To create a business for the owner, instead of a job that only pays him when he works.

Remember:

Employees do their job and get paid. Some business owners have employee mentality. They have jobs within their business and get paid for that. The only way these people can increase their income is to see more guests themselves. Smart business owners *really do* own their business. They get profits because they created recipes. Recipes that ensure the business Intention is delivered each and every time a guest visits, regardless of whether the owners are there or not. In other words, their Intention is delivered **with or without them**. This means the business owner has choice.

So these are the basics. The pillars to take your guests on a Voyage: a journey from pain to rebuilding, and finally to the edge of lifestyle chiropractic. Each of these phases has its own recipe book, of course. We have spent years perfecting ours. The recipes are designed to bring our true Intention to the guest. They are in place to ensure every guest receives our Intention each and every time they visit us.

We recommend you invest plenty of time and energy in creating your recipe book too.

WAKE UP CALL

- Your guests deserve a great chiropractic and customer care experience every time they visit.
- Guests drop off care because they did not feel valued, appreciated, educated and inspired (even if they tell you it is due to money).
- Don't leave the guests' chiropractic and customer experience to chance or personalities. Create recipes and a compelling Voyage.

ACTION POINT

Describe the Voyage of a guest through your practice 'funnel'. List all of the steps including the practice 'touches':

____

____

____

____

____

Identify the 'holes' in the plug that sits at the bottom of your practice 'funnel':

____

____

____

____

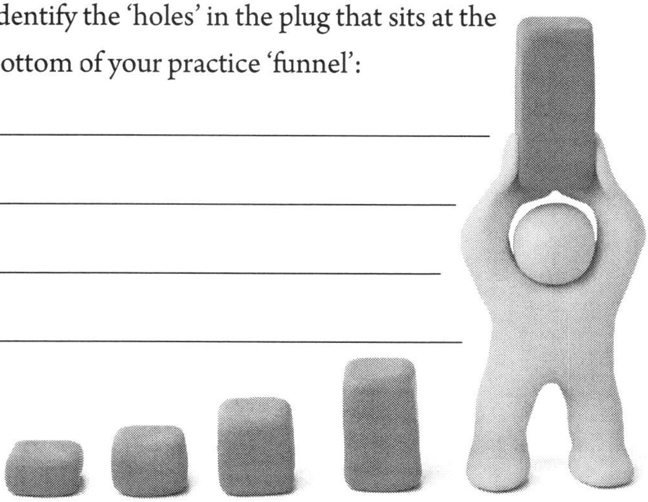

4

VISIBILITY

'Customer experience is the new advertising department.'

MAX KALEHOFF

All over the world there are chiropractors who are clinically great but have empty practices. Without guests to serve, they become frustrated, disillusioned and often bitter. When chiropractors graduate from chiropractic school, they will have passed exams in anatomy, the sciences, psychology, chiropractic philosophy, pathology and so on. But they are seldom taught the reality of attracting new guests and educating them so that they stay in the practice long enough to experience the true benefits of chiropractic.

The problem is this. It could be suggested that chiropractic colleges and universities (particularly in the UK) appear to be desperate to be accepted by the medical profession. They are blind to (or choose not to see) the glaring reality. They base their chiropractic courses on the medical educational model. On the one hand this is fine. The basic education in anatomy, physiology, the life sciences and so on is sound. On the other hand, the chiropractic graduate is ill-equipped to deal with life on the other side of his degree. Unlike his medical colleagues, the chiropractor is thrown into the world with no job guarantee, no knowledge of real practice marketing, no direct support, nowhere to go and often no one to turn to. He is on the edge of the mainstream and is often marginalised by the medical profession chiropractic colleges are so desperate to please. His medical colleagues (graduating at the same time as him) will go into a profession in which a job is virtually guaranteed; where they have the most powerful advertising agency in the world to back them (the pharmaceutical industry); they are joining an established profession that sits at the very heart of Western society; they are becoming part of the mainstream.

If colleges told the truth to their students instead of pretending that they are the 'same' as medics, it might not come as such a shock to them when they graduate. At the very least, they would be disavowed of the belief that they can put a sign over their door that reads, 'Chiropractor', and have the world beating it down in a couple of weeks.

Often the most gifted chiropractors are the least busy in practice. Every chiropractor (gifted or not) must make it his goal to go out and find guests, become important in his community, and take necessary steps to be noticed rather than waiting to be discovered. The steps in this book, if taken faithfully, will certainly get you noticed!

Be aware also that becoming *visible* in your community (and outside it) is the fourth step in the *Crack It!* process. It is not first or second or third. But fourth. There is a good reason for this. Chiropractors who ask us for advice are often most preoccupied with attracting more new guests into their practice. However, without a solid Culture, or a solid team and a firm idea of the Voyage that will be undertaken when new guests arrive, there is no point in becoming visible. The practice cannot serve those new guests who do come in in a way they deserve.

Building And Keeping Your Practice Busy

Building a busy practice and keeping it that way should not be left to chance. It is a military operation which needs a strong set of recipes for success. The great news is that, once you have put the systems in place, they become cyclic.

Your Ideal Guest

When it comes to filling your practice with guests, one thing chiropractors often forget to consider is who their ideal guests actually are. For example, if you are passionate about adjusting sports people, you should be promoting yourself in this area and not in the local old people's home! If you love caring for kids and pregnant ladies, you need to do your research and find out where these potential guests hang out – be sure to arrange a talk at your local NCT group and put your flyers in Starbucks! All of this may sound obvious, but do take the ideal guest question seriously. Often chiropractors are so desperate to build their list that they feel they never have the luxury to narrow their market. To niche it down. This is not true. Three years into practice, Jo came to the decision that she really only wanted to see babies, kids and her *'oldie but goodie'* guests who had been with her from the start and whom she loved to adjust. She styled herself as 'The Baby Chiropractor', and very soon attracted more and more young people to her list. Within twelve months, her practice was at sixty-five per cent under sixteen years of age. At eighteen months, that had increased to eighty-five per cent. Her adjusting rooms were full of babies, mums, grandparents, kids, young teenagers, and guests she had known for ages. She had never been so happy in practice!

Pillars Of Visibility

Your practice's Visibility, its presence in your community, will depend greatly on your Vibe. On the feeling your practice leaves your guests with. On your Culture. That much has been established already (we hope!). That is the central pillar of marketing your practice. A great experience will be passed on by your guests to others. Remember, they will pass on the *feeling* they experienced more than anything else. That is not to denigrate your chiropractic skills. They will have to be good. You have to know your 'chops', as they say. But that is the least we would expect of you!

Outstanding experiences passed on will enhance your Visibility. They do not provide instant gratification (an instant influx of new guests), but they are a very solid provider of new guests in the medium to long term.

So, let's assume you have completed the first three steps on the *Crack It!* process. What about the formal job of making yourself visible? Well, first there are two Visibility strategies. Or at least there used to be. They are internal and external strategies. Any practice, any *business* will feed off of a combination of both of these. However, there is a third strategy which is not exclusively external, and not exclusively internal either. We will talk about this in a moment.

For now, let's consider what the differences are between external and internal strategies:

External Strategies	Internal Strategies
community talks (PA)	health talks (PA)
spinal checks (PA)	spinal checks (PA)
newspaper articles	practice open days (PA)
local radio interviews (PA)	newsletter
	members' parties (PA)
	referrals
	discount vouchers in rooms
	white board education

The letters 'PA' refer to the words 'personal appearance', as mentioned earlier. We will talk more about that in a moment too. First let's look at some of the steps (and the mind set) you must adopt to implement a solid Visibility campaign.

1. Get your head around the fact that you are going to have to leave your practice and get pro-active!
2. If you hate talking in public, join Toastmasters.
3. Get your team involved too!
4. Research your community – find sports centres, uncover shopping malls, schools, clubs, county fairs,

country shows, craft fairs, garden shows, dog shows, make contact with your local radio station, your local newspaper, the library, NCT groups, clubs, WI.

5. Send them a letter or call them up to arrange either a free talk, or for a stand at their event.
6. Book your calendar full to the brim!
7. Your and your team's job is to ensure that you do not remain a well-kept secret!
8. Make one of your team your marketing person who is responsible for booking all the leads that your team creates, and get them to write them down on a large wall calendar where everyone in the team can see them.

Then get another volunteer to help compile the monthly internal promotions. These are events or newsletters or talks that will help get your message to your existing guests.

Let's consider three strategies that have brought our practice great success over the years.

a. WOW! Referral System

WOW! referral is not left to chance. Most people – most of your guests – will not think to refer someone to you unless that person specifically asks them if they know a chiropractor. Your job is to enthuse your guests so that they tell everyone they meet about you! Enthusiastic guests will refer. Not necessarily the ones who have got the best results from your centre. Remember, we are talking about a *feeling*.

The Referral Voucher

We have referral gift vouchers available throughout the centre which are given out during the day to guests. If a new guest arrives as a referral from one of our current guests, we do the following:

a) Ensure the new guest sees the same DC as the person doing the referring.

b) Acknowledge the referrer to the new guest.

c) Send a thank you card to the person who did the referring.

d) Send them a discount voucher for a service within our practice – *Hot Stone Massage,* for example – a true want purchase!

e) Put a referral celebration board out each month saying, 'HUGE thanks to the following people for referring their friends and family to us during the month of ...' Then we list their first names and the names of the people they referred.

This process helps both the referrer and the new guest become even more enthusiastic about us, as we thank them for helping us to spread our particular chiropractic message. It is a great social proof tool too.

Remember, this is not an exercise in pressurising people to visit your practice. All you can and should do is be passionate about your Intention – your Intention for them and your practice. That's it. We always say to our potential referrers: *'You cannot force people to come in, but we are very grateful to you for telling your friends and giving them our vouchers.'*

Chiropractors are sometimes afraid of asking for referrals – don't be! Interact and educate guests and they will become your biggest marketing tool. Talk talk talk about chiropractic!

b. What's The Story Morning Glory?

Create stories around your practice. Not made-up stories, but 'camp-fire' stories that are true and that all the team and the guests know about. The story might be about the history of your practice, it might be about how you got into chiropractic, or even about the day your life was changed by chiropractic.

Ours are about how we started in a tiny room in a sports centre, and grew to a fourteen-room wellness centre that serves thousands of guests in our community. About how our lifestyle membership was started at the request of a guest nine years ago (he was our first gold member and is a very active member still!). About Starbucks. We have a history wall depicting the stages of our practice growth. The wall includes pictures of team members and guests who have been important in our development.

Guests love to be part of something like this. It creates community. Family. But only if it is *genuine*. Do not implement these strategies if you do not *feel* them.

So what's your story?

c. WOW! Guest Story Book

Another great internal promotion is the guest story book. The story book is the chance for your guests to tell their chiropractic story. They don't have to gush or 'big-up' or sell you and your services to anyone. They just need to tell the truth: how they felt, what happened to them and how they are feeling now. Our guests are drawn to the story books time and time again. Especially the books of their own chiropractor. There are photos, jokes, stories and tidbits in them that encourage the chiropractor's connection with the guest and vice versa. Story books also help guests 'see behind the curtain', which helps build a relationship-centred practice.

d. The Personal Appearance

The personal appearance has provided us with an avalanche of new guests over the years. There is nothing quite like it. Not to do PAs is to deny your practice hundreds and hundreds of new guests.

PAs are an occasion when you (or one of your team) 'personally appear' at an event. It might be a talk or a spinal screen, or it might be a lecture of some kind. Any occasion in which the public get to interact with you personally. This personal contact is probably the most powerful tool in attracting new guests to your practice. By 'new guests', we mean those who have not been referred and who have had no previous contact with you either directly or indirectly.

A PA allows people to interact with you in a way that cannot be done through any other medium. PAs are always more compelling than anything else. Think of your favourite singer, for instance. Listening to their record is enjoyable, seeing them in concert is a different experience entirely. It is much more powerful. A PA helps a potential new guest feel your passion and your Intention. Remember, almost all communication is non-verbal. Communication is about your body language. It's about your tonality. It's about your energy and commitment. Can they trust you? Are you an expert? Can you get them well? These questions are rattling around in a potential new guest's head when they move into your orbit. They are easily resolved with a PA.

Remember, again, about the perception of what you do. Chiropractic is not promoted to the public. It is not established in their minds (yet!). They have not been subjected to advertising (subliminal or otherwise) extolling its virtues; promoting its benefits. Unlike mainstream medicine, for instance. For that reason, PAs allow the chiropractor to take his message straight to those who will benefit from hearing it.

Like everything else, PAs must be planned. There must be a recipe that dictates how your PAs are carried out and what happens during them. What message are you trying to convey? What will you say when a potential new guest approaches you? These things should not be left to chance. There are effective ways of communicating your message – clear and concise methods of putting it across. There are ineffective ways too. Think about how you will do it. How you will represent your Intention. There should be a process to any interaction with a potential new guest. A series of steps that should be taken. They should never be skipped or skimmed over.

PAs are more powerful than any other marketing tool for new guests. We have used PAs frequently throughout our practice build. In fact PAs built the foundation of our practice!

Website And Social Media

We have left this subject to last, and have done so for a number of reasons. First because we believe that your website and your social media presence do not fit snugly into a straight external Visibility strategy or a straight internal Visibility strategy. Instead, they sit somewhere in between. We'll expand on this in a moment.

The second reason to leave it to last is because the Internet and social media's power has only recently been recognised by 'offline' businesses, especially those marketing to their local community. For a long time, chiropractors thought that an Internet presence was more suited to a business that did not rely on clients coming from a specific locale. Not that chiropractors didn't have websites, most did. But with the decline of *Yellow Pages*, chiropractic websites were (and still are) not much more than a fuller version of their old *Yellow Pages* entry. In other words, they are 'information' sites. They are crammed with content that extols the virtues of chiropractic and the chiropractic lifestyle; that gives information about conditions and complaints and techniques, and how the profession is regulated. They have 'stock' photographs of 'well' people. Finally, they encourage the 'browsing' mentality. They are reference centres. Mini-*Wiki* sites. They rarely encourage the browser to take action. To proactively seek your services.

In other words, there is little *emotion* in them. No *feeling*. No *Culture* for the guest to latch on to or have a reaction to.

There are specific strategies that a chiropractor's website must have. Ninety per cent of it should be about the stuff that is almost always overlooked. We call this the *OK!* stuff. *OK! Magazine* (in the UK) is full of pictures, snippets of gossip from 'celebs', and people you think you 'might' know but can't quite place. The magazine is all about feeling. It has no news value, there is no learning in it, it goes nowhere. What it does do is *connect*. That's why it sells! Your website should be much more like *OK!*

Social Media

Your website and your social media presence are attractive to both your existing guests and potential new guests. If your website and your social media sites are interactive, if they change regularly and connect with guests, then your existing guests will be just as attracted to them as new ones. This is why we believe your web presence is neither external nor internal in terms of Visibility. It sits somewhere in between. A virtual office that never closes but is always connecting with your guests, old and new. This is real power!

Social media allows you to have long conversations with people who care about what you do. You can talk directly to your 'market' for almost no cost. Social media and your web presence should generate enquiries into your practice. Sites like Wordpress, Twitter and Facebook are great for this. So is your home page (if it is interactive). If it touches the visitor in some way. An 'information site' just won't do it. Social media also allows you to create a strong brand for your practice. A consistent message about who you are and what you stand for.

SEO And Becoming 'Google-able'

When you search on Google for someone important, someone visible, someone who is 'making a dent' on the universe, there is usually a bunch of stuff that comes up: articles, photos, videos, their website, and their social media pages. That is because the important people are using the 'must-use' sites to make them web-famous. Google loves these sites and rates the information on them very highly.

The sites we are talking about include:

- YouTube
- Slideshare
- Facebook
- LinkedIn
- Ecademy

- Wordpress
- Twitter

If you embrace these sites, if you have a presence on them and update them regularly, Google will truly love you! Your guests, your friends and followers will love you too, because they can quickly connect with your Intention and your Culture through your videos, photos, groups and articles. It's important to remember, however, that your success both on and offline will only be as good as your *Intention*. If your message isn't strong, you'll be wasting your time and, worse, you might be damaging your brand.

So embrace the net, re-imagine your website and think deeply about your social media strategy. Then, when you are ready to see how to make all of this work pay off, turn the page for the final step in the *Crack It!* process.

WAKE UP CALL

- High visibility is a combination of internal and external strategies that should not be left to chance.
- Fill your wall planner up with both in January for the year ahead.
- Surround yourself with team members who love PAs (with or without you). If you are attending and they are not, you have the wrong team!
- Visibility is a team effort.
- Keeping your practice full is easy with a plan.

ACTION POINT

Imagine your ideal guest. Describe them (young, old, sporty, financially challenged or solvent):

List the internal and external strategies you currently employ:

List others you will now start using:

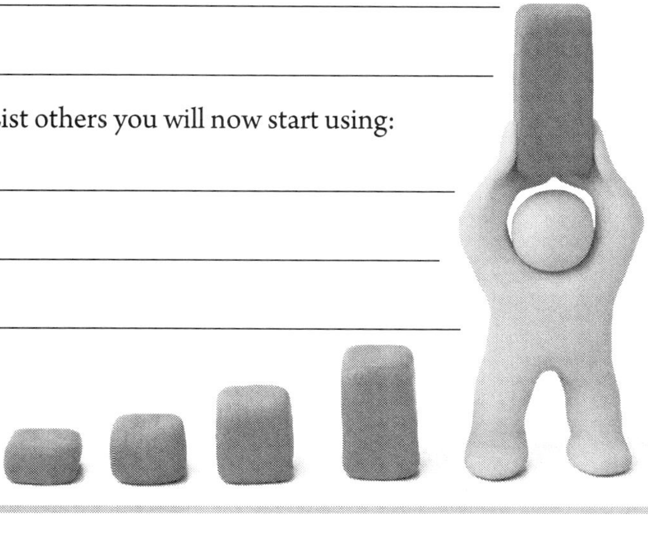

5

VISCERAL

'The doctor of the future will give no medicine, but will interest her or his patients in the care of the human frame, in a proper diet, and in the cause and prevention of disease.'

THOMAS EDISON

Visceral is the last step of the *Crack It!* process. The dictionary describes visceral as: *'characterised by or proceeding from instinct rather than intellect: a visceral reaction.'* This effect is something that your practice should be aiming to have over your guests. We don't mean some brain-washing mumbo-jumbo, but a pure intent to appeal to their emotion – to their instinct rather than their intellect.

Let's give you an example of what we mean by this. We'd like to introduce you to an accountant. More specifically to *our* accountant. We haven't been with him long, but in the short time we have been together, he has answered all our questions around expertise and trust. He has over-delivered. He is always available, he is keen and has great energy. He is excited about our business. It's genuine too. We don't believe you can fake stuff like that! How do you think we *feel* about him?

Well, he makes us feel *good,* that's for sure. He makes us feel secure in the knowledge that an expert is taking care of our financial obligations. He gives us direction, expertise and trust. In fact, he has become a *part* of our business. He would have to do something seriously awful for us to consider finding another accountant. In other words, he has (in a short period of time) become *visceral.*

Was he unethical? Did he brainwash us or use NLP on us, or coerce us into doing things we didn't want to do? Did he manipulate us? Of course not! He was outstanding in his interactions with us. He understood our needs, our desires, our fears, and made sure he over-delivered.

That is what we are talking about when we speak of a chiropractic centre that is Visceral. If you cast your mind back to our Voyage funnel, we described the plug with holes in it that sits at the bottom of the funnel. Well, the more Visceral your practice is, the fewer holes there are in the plug.

What we are describing here is the last stage of the Voyage: **VP4.** Guests will embark on VP4 if chiropractic has become a part of their lifestyle. If *you* have become part of their *lives.* If your practice (and the guest's decision to visit it) has become a Visceral decision.

Once your guests have completed their initial course of care, they should not only be pain-free, they should have started a gentle exercise programme and, in our case, have completed a 'rebuild your back' programme. In our centres, they are more than likely to have been assessed for orthotics, to have started regular chiropractic massage and improved their diet. They will know about our philosophy and understand what our practice is striving to achieve. In turn, we will have got to know them well. We now understand them in terms of their life, their family, their wants, their needs and, ultimately, their long term health aim. We are invested in them and they are invested in us. We have embarked, in other words, on the relationship-chiropractic model that is part of our Intention. Our task now is to determine the level of chiropractic they want as a part of their lifestyle.

Some people never want to have chiropractic again until they are in pain once more. They prefer to have another course of sessions to help their symptoms only. That's fine. Others prefer to have lifestyle chiropractic. That is, on-going chiropractic adjustments that maintain optimum spinal health. We have always advocated this approach for ourselves and our family. It felt good, we remained healthier, fitter and more positive because of it. There is a good amount of research that backs this up too. Read *Functional Anatomy Of The Spine* by Middleditch and Oliver, for instance, and the explanation on why intervertebral discs degenerate. Or the brand new paper (at the time of writing) in the prestigious *Spine* journal called, *'Does maintained Spinal manipulation therapy for chronic non-specific low back pain result in better long term outcome?' (Senna MK, Machaly SA, 2011).* We won't go in to it too much here but would encourage you to read widely.

So we believe in relationship chiropractic. We believe you should have a firm place in your guest's life, like a supportive, loving friend who will do anything to help them. And you will, won't you? That's certainly our promise to our guests.

We have been asked hundreds of times about our membership approach to chiropractic. Many people have told us they want to 'copy' it. There has been a lot of wrong speculation about it. The membership was not designed to *'sign 'em up'* or to *'keep 'em coming'*, neither was it designed like a membership to a gym. Our lifestyle membership is the opposite of this. We have a membership because we want people to be able to have regular chiropractic care and pay less the longer they have been enjoying a relationship with us. We want them to feel part of our family, part of our community. We want them to enjoy pro-active health instead of symptom-chasing, reactive health. The membership is an important part of our Culture. Without the Culture, membership becomes a different experience.

So we advise anyone to work on their Culture before they set up any form of membership. That is why Intention and Culture is the first step in the *Crack It!* process. Without the correct Intention, membership is lifeless and its benefits are lost. The members must also be in line with the Intention and Culture. It must speak to them. Inspire them.

Members experience extra special guest care too. Priority booking, specific newsletters, members' parties, get-togethers, and they attend lectures in our practice on all things health and well-being. They enjoy discounted chiropractic care and massage. They become part of a 'Guests' Association' that supports new guests. They, in turn, are supported by their fellow Association members. We love them being part of our family.

Let's tell you how the membership came about. It began because of these words in our Intention Statement: *'... we offer lifetime care to all who seek our services ...'*

We puzzled over how to bring this to our guests, other than with an offer of continued care where they would come to us sporadically, the onus being on them to remember and on us to keep our relationship alive. We wanted people to get adjusted in the same way that we got adjusted.

The 'light-bulb' moment was highlighted by a discussion Steve had with one of his guests back in 2002. Steve was talking about lifestyle chiropractic and how often the guest wanted to get adjusted, with a recommendation that the guest returned in six weeks.

The guest asked Steve, 'How often do you get adjusted?'

Steve said, 'Weekly.'

The guest then asked, 'How about Jo?'

Steve replied, 'Weekly.'

The guest continued, 'How often do your parents get adjusted?'

Steve shrugged, 'Whenever they want, depending on what they've been up to. Normally weekly.'

Then the guest said something which would transform our thinking forever: 'If your family get adjusted whenever they like and you get adjusted weekly, why are you advising me to come in six weeks? Why are you not recommending the same for me as you are for your own family?'

There was silence in the adjusting room.

We pondered the answer later that evening. It really came down to one thing – *money*. Steve didn't want to appear as 'pushy' or 'money-grabbing', so he recommended a level of care that was cheaper, but that he did not believe in himself. So we had to change the money barrier. Some guests, of course, would happily pay full price each time they visited, whereas others were not in a position to do this. We felt we would rather charge less and enable more people to have chiropractic whenever they wanted. Our Intention was to offer 'lifetime care for everyone who sought it'.

We decided on two types of membership:

GOLD – for guests who wanted chiropractic as *we* had chiropractic, ie whenever they chose.

SILVER – for people who wanted to get adjusted once a month.

There was no fee to join the lifestyle membership. When we started, we set up a standing order system, which moved to direct debit as the numbers of members grew.

Highlights Of Our Membership Recipe

- Guests must have completed their initial course of care.
- Guests are not 'hard sold' into joining membership.
- There is no joining fee.

- Guests sign a direct debit form which will mean their payment comes out on 1st of the month.
- We have a membership co-ordinator who is responsible for checking the statements and compiling a membership list each month.
- People are still given a normal receipt if they want one.
- Members have their own coloured appointments on the computer system to distinguish them from other guests.
- Unlike gym memberships, members do not sign up for a year. We believe that chiropractic care is a choice, so they get all the benefits of membership, but can leave at any time they wish.
- Members have their appointments booked in advance so that they can secure their ideal time. If we didn't prebook them, they would not get their ideal time.
- By booking their appointments in advance, we can give them a list in September for the following year, so when they get their new calendars, the first thing that goes on them are their chiropractic appointments. We and our members see chiropractic as deserving priority place in their lives.

There is no aspect of our membership which is about 'hard sell' and tying people into having chiropractic care. This goes against our Intention. It is always a choice. Building an ethical, membership-based practice is also great for your business. We have a practice that is half-full with raving fans before any promotion is undertaken; before the new week begins; before we do anything else. We get to adjust a list full of people who love chiropractic the way we administer it. They want to make it a priority in their life. We are adjusting our 'family'.

Because of the membership, our practice is full of guests who love what we do and love being adjusted by us. From a financial standpoint, there is also the security for the practice, of course. But more than that, members are chiropractic advocates who love the *context* in which we deliver chiropractic. The energy, therefore, is always high in our centres.

Over time, our membership (and our business) has grown and grown in line with our Intention. The buoyancy of our membership has always reflected the group dynamic. It surges forwards at times of high energy, of enthusiasm, of positive advocacy. It stutters if we are not completely (as a group) living up to our exceptional standards.

Summary Of Benefits Of Lifestyle Membership

- Proactive approach to spinal health.
- A loving, supportive environment in which to grow.
- A network of like-minded guests.
- Discounted chiropractic care.
- Priority appointments.
- Members' discounts on other services.
- Members' newsletter.
- Members' summer and Christmas parties.
- Guests become part of our community.
- Guests join our Guest Association (a support association to help new and not-so-new guests).
- Guests are invited to bi-monthly talks in the practice given by a variety of speakers (including other healthcare professionals, fitness experts, weight loss professionals, nutritional experts. The list of interesting speakers is endless!).
- Ultimately the guest has a cost effective way to enjoy lifestyle chiropractic.

Benefits To The Chiropractic Business

- A practice full of chiropractic advocates who love to have chiropractic as part of their lifestyle.
- Pre booked guests.
- Membership fees coming into the centre every month via S/O or D/D.
- The practice creates a community of lifestyle members.
- It is great fun adjusting and caring for practice advocates.

The transition from initial care to lifestyle chiropractic should be a seamless one. It is the next step for those who are attracted to what you do. If your Intention is strong, if it is honest and speaks of your highest ideals, then the majority of your guests will want to continue their relationship with it. Not a relationship with *you* necessarily, but with your *Intention* and, as an extension of that, your *Culture*. The way you do this will be in your lifestyle membership recipe book, along with everything else.

WAKE UP CALL

- Build a community within your practice that your guests and team want to stay part of.
- 'Hard selling' or 'patient contracts' or fear tactics do not create community.
- Membership is about creating a passionate, vibrant community. It is not about 'sign ups'.
- The community will actively refer more people like themselves.

ACTION POINT

What does Visceral mean to you?

Consider your practice community. List five steps you can take to make it more Visceral:

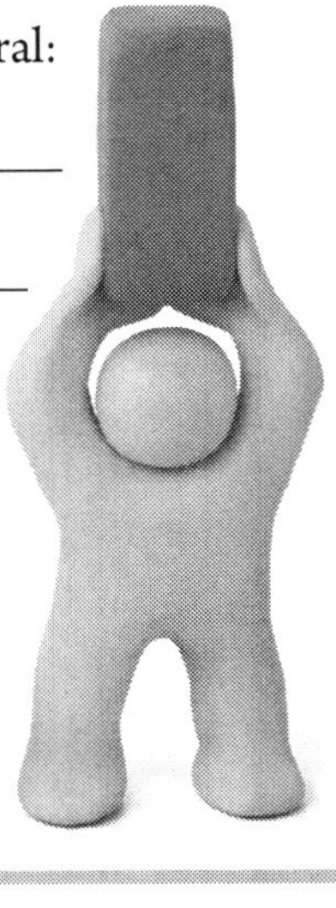

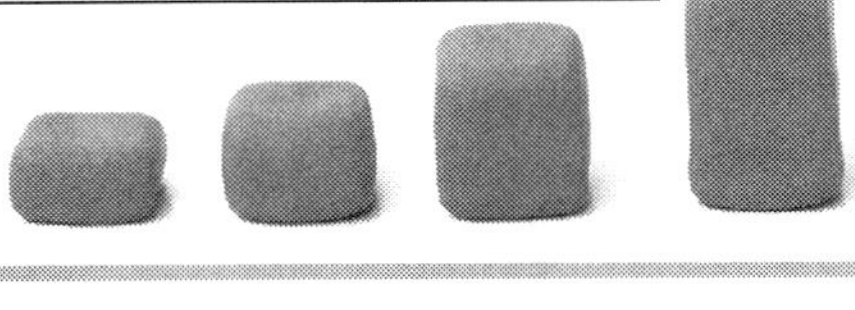

JUST DO IT!

'A journey of a thousand miles begins with a single step.'

LAO-TZU

So there you have it. The last step in the *Crack It!* process. The fifth step in creating a WOW! practice. This five-step formula is the same one we used to build our practice from a single, tiny room in a sports leisure centre, to a million pound practice with a Starbucks coffee house in our welcome area! Then we used the five-step process again to build an outstanding smaller practice in a small town. We have achieved this honestly, ethically and with great joy. To do it has been a wondrous journey filled with great team-mates and super guests who have now become life-long friends. We hope in reading this you will be inspired to implement the process and take action.

The Seven Big Mistakes To Avoid

Mistakes are a part of business. We all make them. We will continue to make them. That's part of the fun. Part of the challenge. Often it's the business mistakes we make that allow us to grow our skills, so they are not a bad thing. However, there are some big mistakes. We have addressed most of them in this book, but chiropractic business owners still make them. They come up time after time. So we want to focus you one last time on what they are. Put them in your face so to speak. We hope you don't mind. There are seven of them.

1. Getting ' stuck' with a job, not a business.
2. Failing to create an Intention for the business.
3. Failing to create a Culture in the practice.
4. Recruiting associates when the business owner is feeling overwhelmed, and paying them fifty per cent.
5. Putting up with receptionists instead of training chiropractic advocates.
6. Failing to create a recipe book in line with the practice Intention that covers every aspect of the business.
7. Failing to 'give service' to guests for life through a relationship-centred chiropractic model.

The steps laid out in this book, the phases of the practice build, are designed to avoid all of these seven. As you might expect, we have made most of the mistakes on the list at one time or another and they were a source of pain and frustration. That's why we are telling you about them one more time – so that you don't have to.

Do This One Thing

From experience, we know that ninety-eight per cent of chiropractors or chiropractic business owners who pick up this book, or those taking our seminars, or taking a programme – any programme no matter who is giving it – will enjoy it, will often agree with it, will hopefully be inspired by it – yet will do nothing with the information. They will not take action. They will do nothing to push their practice and their life forwards. And they'll all have a story as to why too. A reason they didn't do it.

Coaching our own team for many years, and coaching independent chiropractors and business owners, means we have heard every conceivable story. Blaming the team for example: *my team wouldn't go for it* ... Or blaming 'patients': *my 'patients' wouldn't like it* ... Or their location: *it would never work where I practise* ... Or there is fear: *I don't want the full package* ... Or plain lack of commitment: *I haven't got around to doing it yet* ... and so on.

There is always a reason – a story – to stop action. To delay it. To procrastinate on it. Don't allow that to happen to you! Don't stifle your growth potential. Don't let 'dream stealers' convince you that you should leave things as they are and not rock the boat. You deserve a WOW practice!

Take the first step. If you do nothing else, do that much. Get the boulder rolling. Rolling towards transformation. It will feel good if you move it just a bit. If it feels good, you will be encouraged to do more of it. If you do more of it – and do it consistently – you will start to make progress!

So if you do nothing else with this information, with these strategies, *set your Intention*. Lay a new foundation. That is why it *is* the first step. The most important step.

Note that point.

Marketing, attracting new guests, implementing 'management systems', taking on team members, learning how to run a health talk and dozens of other 'skills' chiropractic business owners believe they must have *are not the first step*.

The Intention is.

Throw yourself into it and produce an Intention Statement that speaks of your joy. Of your passion. Of what you want to see in the world. Then live in line with it. Do it every day in your practice. Insist everyone else does the same. Champion it. Drive it forwards and never, ever let it down. Not intentionally at least (no pun intended!).

If you do this much, you will be well on your way to creating a practice of your dreams. A life you could hardly have imagined. You will change your community. You will transform your team and, more importantly, you will transform yourself. You will indeed have created a WOW! chiropractic practice. You deserve it!

We wish you love, luck and transformation on the journey in front of you. If you undertake it – if you truly undertake it – if you fully immerse yourself in it, it will be the most exciting experience of your life. It will transform your life, your loved ones, your team, your guests, and a new world of chiropractic shall be unleashed. Take it from us.

About Jo and Steve

Ten years ago, Jo and Steve Davison created and developed a unique chiropractic business in the south-east of England. The success of this meant they were soon in demand to consult and teach their strategies to chiropractors throughout the UK. This grew and now they are helping chiropractors globally. They created *Crack It!* to deliver a five-step process to chiropractors wanting to create their own WOW! practice.

Jo and Steve have a passion for helping chiropractors create a practice of their dreams. One in which they free themselves from being 'jobbing chiropractors' who happen to own the practice (often working harder and getting paid less than they did as associates), living on a knife-edge, stressed and working far too hard to keep it all going, to becoming *chiropractic business owners* and manifesting their dream life. Creating opportunities for themselves and those around them.

What people say about Jo and Steve and Crack It!

'Jo and Steve seemed like the ideal people to turn to when business became difficult to deal with. They have given me the boost I needed to carry on developing my chiropractic clinic, at a time when I was thinking of quitting chiropractic completely. Their friendly, professional, passionate, highly motivated/ motivating nature, alongside some fantastic practical advice have helped to set me on the right track again. I would thoroughly recommend their services. Their down to earth yet highly inspirational approach are a must for all business owners, and anyone that wants to reach their full potential in life.'

Dr Mandy Hensman DC,
Chiropractor and Business Owner

'What makes a good coach? Credibility, experience, confidence, enthusiasm, creativity, sensitivity and vision. Jo and Steve have all of this and more. They have demonstrated in their own personal and professional lives that their approach works, and that it can be adapted to your personal requirements. I have recommended their services before and will continue to send them referrals for coaching. With their help you can take your professional and personal dreams to the next level and even beyond what you can currently imagine. I know I will continue to work with them on an ongoing basis, if for no other reason then to just hang out with them and share the passion.'

Dr Cherye Roche DC, Aukland, New Zealand

'Steve and Jo have the unique ability to motivate you beyond what you thought possible! Once they've helped you to figure out your direction (even if you don't know it!) you can expect imaginative, innovative, inspiring coaching to shift your boundaries and help you to reach the goals you want to achieve. The discovery and learning with Steve and Jo is endless as they help you grow and become the very best you can be. For me, the coaching was invaluable and it continues to be every day.'

Dr Jo Ladd DC, Chiropractor

'Jo and Steve run their clinic with vision and they create a dynamic environment that has a beneficial effect on everyone around them. My life has totally turned around since meeting them. I used to consider myself as one of life's victims and I had resigned myself to always having bad luck. Jo, particularly, has turned my way of thinking totally upside down. She gave me the tools to make things happen both personally and professionally. I now understand how to successfully set myself short-term achievable goals that build towards the fulfillment of my longer-term dreams. Also, with the renewed vigour and positive behaviour that has resulted from this turn around has come ever greater energy to accelerate this process at an even greater speed.'

Emma Whipp MT

'Having trained with Jo and Steve, I subsequently was lucky enough to locum for them at various stages of their professional development. During that time I have become an admirer of their approach to business. Their consultation and advice have been more valuable than most as they really have "been there and done it", and tried many avenues to work out a successful route in business.'

Dr Ed Groenhart DC, Radcliffe on Trent

'Jo and Steve were amazing mentors. As well as learning so much more about chiropractic and business I also grew tremendously as a person. They took me completely out of my comfort zone and never stopped motivating and believing in me. I had the best start in the profession with their coaching and can't imagine what I would be like without that. They are the most inspirational couple that I have ever met. Thanks for everything.'

Dr Paula Garcia DC, Chiropractor

'The best coaching for chiropractors in the UK. Inspiring, educational supportive, bespoke information to suit all motivated chiropractors.'

Dr Andrew Goddard DC CBO, Anglia Chiropractic, UK

'I have got so much from the Crack it process! It has transformed my thinking and business more than I ever anticipated. Thanks Jo and Steve!'

Dr Shelley Irving DC CBO, UK

‘To run a chiropractic clinic you need more than adjusting skills but where do you start? If you want a bunch of advice put together by someone else and then reproduced by your staff Crack-It is not for you. If you want to develop yourself as a leader, business owner and entrepreneur by understanding the essentials and being supported by the top two Gurus in the field. To have a network of likeminded people to hold you accountable when you embark on the journey to design your bespoke Dream Practice based on your values and your intentions in life, Crack-It will help you step by step. Your chiropractic future will be instantly more exciting and rewarding.’

Dr Mats Hansson DC, Hansson Chiropractic, Weymouth, UK

‘Jo and Steve have enabled me to transform from an anxious, self doubting Chiropractor to a driven, focused and empowered CBO. The Crack it! universe is full of amazing, supportive, fellow Chiropractors. What Jo and Steve have created is one of a kind and a community like no other. I am so grateful to be part of it and highly recommend this process. Full of gratitude.’

Dr Angel Koonar Turner DC CBO, Essex, UK

‘Crack it! has had a life changing effect on me! The process has given me purpose and self esteem. Thank you Jo and Steve for your insight, wisdom and encouragement.’

Sarah Simpson CBO, UK

'Crack it is amazing! It has helped me to see that I was not running a business, I was working hard with 'staff' who were not inspired. Jo and Steve have an amazing programme that will help you get from where you are to where you want to go, presented in a down to earth way with no gimmicks. They have created a great community that will support you in this process with other motivated Chiro's and Osteo's'.

Paul Musk DO OBO, London, UK

'Jo and Steve – Thank you so much! This process has really given us confidence to pursue our dreams and start a practice of our own!'

Richard and Catriona Anthony CBOs, UK

'I want to say a HUGE thank you to Jo and Steve for helping me step up and become a better business owner. The process has allowed me to get strong with my vision and mindset'.

Dr Rebecca Ashby DC CBO, UK

'Looking to step away from the coal face of your practise and really take control as a chiropractic business owner. Well crack it is for you. In their book, Jo and Steve, will take you to a totally new level to help transform your practise, business and life. Read on ...'

Dr Carl Irwin DC CBO, London, UK

'Jo and Steve, through their Crack It process have reminded me that I had a big vision however I'd become distracted by the daily running of my clinic. Their coaching and guidance is invaluable for all Chiropractic business owners, especially if you feel overwhelmed, have little to no management training and you're working a crazy amount of hours! Their support and guidance shows you can be a winner!

Does it work? ... Definitely. Is it worth it? ... Absolutely!

Much love and thanks to Jo and Steve for their love and support. They really deliver the WOW!'

Dr Julia Pullin DC CBO, UK

'Jo and steve have helped us to transform our business and our lives. I can't recommend them highly enough. The crackit mentorship program has taken us from the brink of burnout and opened our minds to the joys of being inspired and enthusiastic chiropractic business owners. They have truly thought of every minut detail all successful business owners need. They support us with such passion and belief that there can only be one outcome, SUCCESS!

I know our lives will never be the same again and now we have the belief that we can achieve anything we desire and the opportunity to dream big!'

Steve Drake CBO, Devon, UK

'Dr Jo Davison has been positively impacting audiences for many years. With her simple yet clear message of choosing to follow your own path and deliver excellence in everything that you do, she engages and challenges her audience to BE at a higher level and then DO at a higher level. In teaching the critical links between personal success and belief systems and professional success, Dr Jo speaks with a passion, certainty and conviction that will empower you to step out of your comfort zone and be the change you wish to see.'

Ross McDonald DC, President of the Scottish Chiropractic Association; Owner, The Edinburgh Lectures Chiropractic Conference

'Jo Davison has spoken for the United Chiropractic Association on many occasions. She is very passionate about creating dream teams and chiropractors having a practice that they love to be in! I know that Jo and her husband Steve have been instrumental in helping many UK chiropractors with their journey to a WOW practice.'

Melissa Sandford
On Behalf of the United Chiropractic Association

Printed in Great Britain
by Amazon

46765083R00102